FOREIGN LANGUAGES
WIPE YOUR FEET
BLEEP! FLEEBLE! SQUONK!
DOGGO BISCUITS
LINGOAPHONE HEADSET
COOKERY
HERE'S SOME I ATE EARLIER!
CHEF
FATTY
SUGAR
RAISINS
SQUEEZE!
ICING BAG
Fatty
£4.50

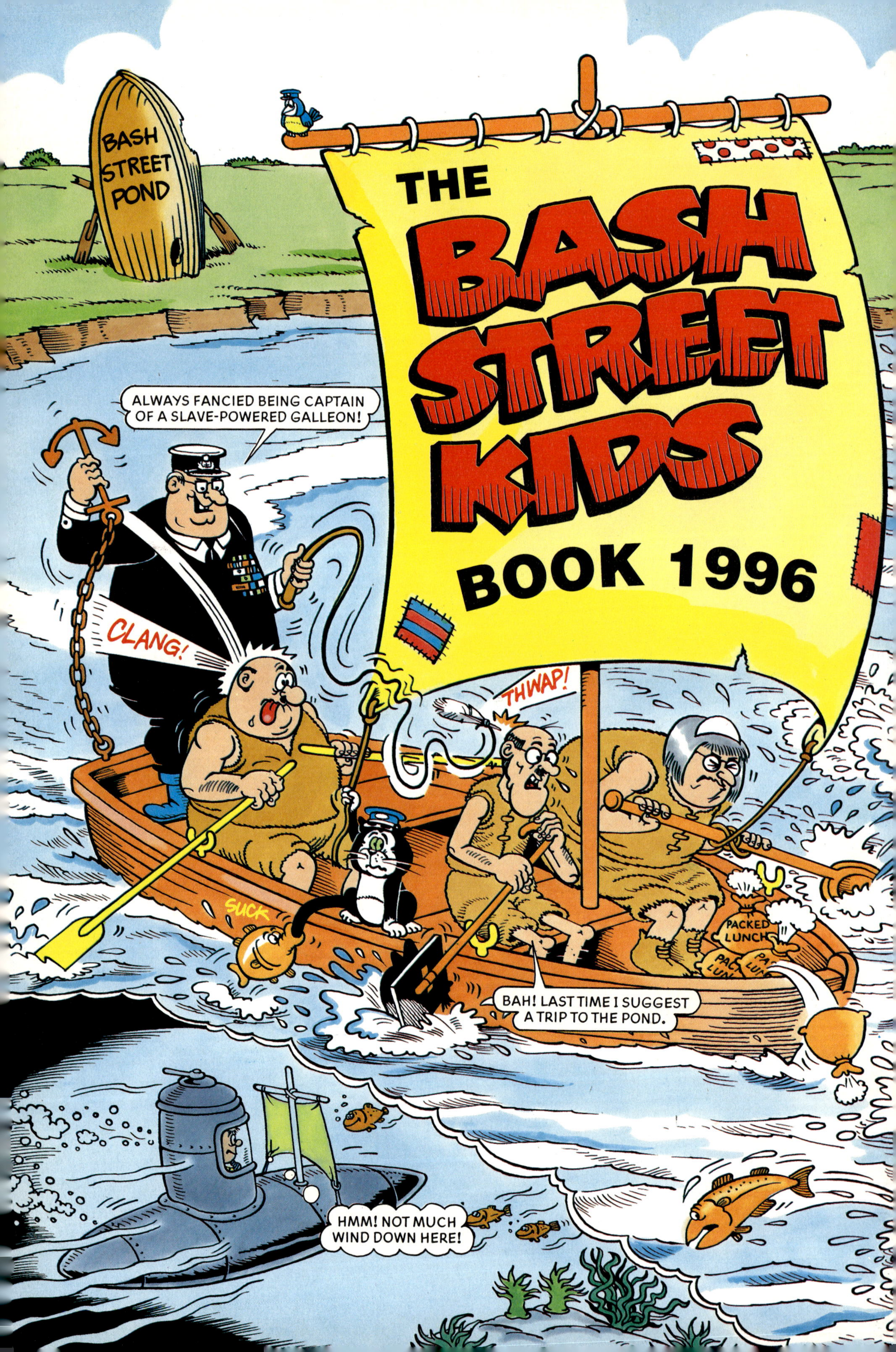
BASH
STREET
POND
THE
BASH
STREET
KIDS
BOOK 1996
ALWAYS FANCIED BEING CAPTAIN
OF A SLAVE-POWERED GALLEON!
CLANG!
THWAP!
SUCK
PACKED
LUNCH
BAH! LAST TIME I SUGGEST
A TRIP TO THE POND.
HMM! NOT MUCH
WIND DOWN HERE!

Printed and Published in Great Britain by D. C. THOMSON & CO., LTD.,
185 Fleet Street, London EC4A 2HS.
 ISBN 0-85116-603-2

CRAFTY BUNCH
CRAFT CLASS TODAY! I LOVE CRAFT CLASS, BECAUSE I'M BRILLIANT AT MAKING THINGS.
Cuthbert Cringeworthy, Teacher's pet.
GROAN!
WE HATE CRAFT CLASS, BECAUSE WE'RE NOT BRILLIANT AT MAKING THINGS!
AND NOW I'M MAKING DANNY SNEEZE!
ERK!
CHOO!
GRR! YOU'RE MAKING CUTHBERT CRY LIKE A LITTLE BABY!
M-MY POOR MODEL! SOB! SNIVEL! WAIL!
CUTHBERT IS A LITTLE BABY!
I CAN USE THIS.
GRR! NOW I'LL HAVE TO GO AND GET DRY!
TEACHER'S ANGRY! WE'LL GET IN HIS GOOD BOOKS, IF WE MAKE SOMETHING GOOD.
So—
ER! PLANK "A" JOINS . . . IT SAYS WE NEED ELASTIC.
I'LL GET IT.
MODEL PLANS
In the boiler house—
. . . IT'S A ROMAN CATAPULT!
PYOING!
OOPS!
SNAP!
Then—
WHO PINCHED MY BRACES?
SO THAT'S WHERE SMIFFY GOT THE ELASTIC.

So—
I'M MAKING THIS MODEL OUT OF WASHING-UP LIQUID BOTTLES AND DOUBLE-SIDED STICKY TAPE.
SHOW-OFF!
I'M MAKING A SNACK.
CREATIVE COOKERY
PLENTY PEPPER! YUMMY!
AHHHH . . .
I'M MAKING A TANK.
VERY GOOD, SMIFFY.
Later—
DOESN'T LOOK MUCH LIKE A TANK TO ME.
OF COURSE IT DOES . . .
. . . IT'S A WATER TANK!
GLUBBLE!
TUG!
SOON BE NICE AND DRY.
Later—
THAT DOESN'T LOOK LIKE A MODEL OF "THE BEANO" EDITOR'S DESK TO ME.
DOESN'T IT?
IT'S AS COMFY AS THE EDITOR'S DESK, THOUGH.
YOU SHORT-SIGHTED TWIT, 'ERBERT! THAT'S NOT A MODEL OF THE DESK . . .
IT ISN'T?
OOO! LUCKY I LANDED ON SOMETHING SOFT — TEACHER'S HEAD!
THUD!
WAH!
YOU'RE MAKING ME MAD! YOU'RE ALL GOING TO . . .
. . . DISAPPEAR? WELL, THE KIDS ARE GOOD AT MAKING SOMETHING— ESCAPES!

Spring Fashions
SEE WHAT I FOUND — WE CAN HAVE FUN WITH THESE.
YOU NEED A SAFETY SPRING LIKE MINE, DANNY — WATCH.
I DON'T SEE ANYTHING SA ABOUT THAT SPRING!
HEAVE!
HOWL!
HOLD IT! IT'S NOT WORKING — I'VE GOT A MUCH BETTER IDEA!
THIS PEPPER SHOULD DO THE TRICK.
AHHH . . .
Then—
ER — MAYBE I DIDN'T HAVE A GOOD IDEA FOR ONCE!
OW!
WALLOP!
YIKES!

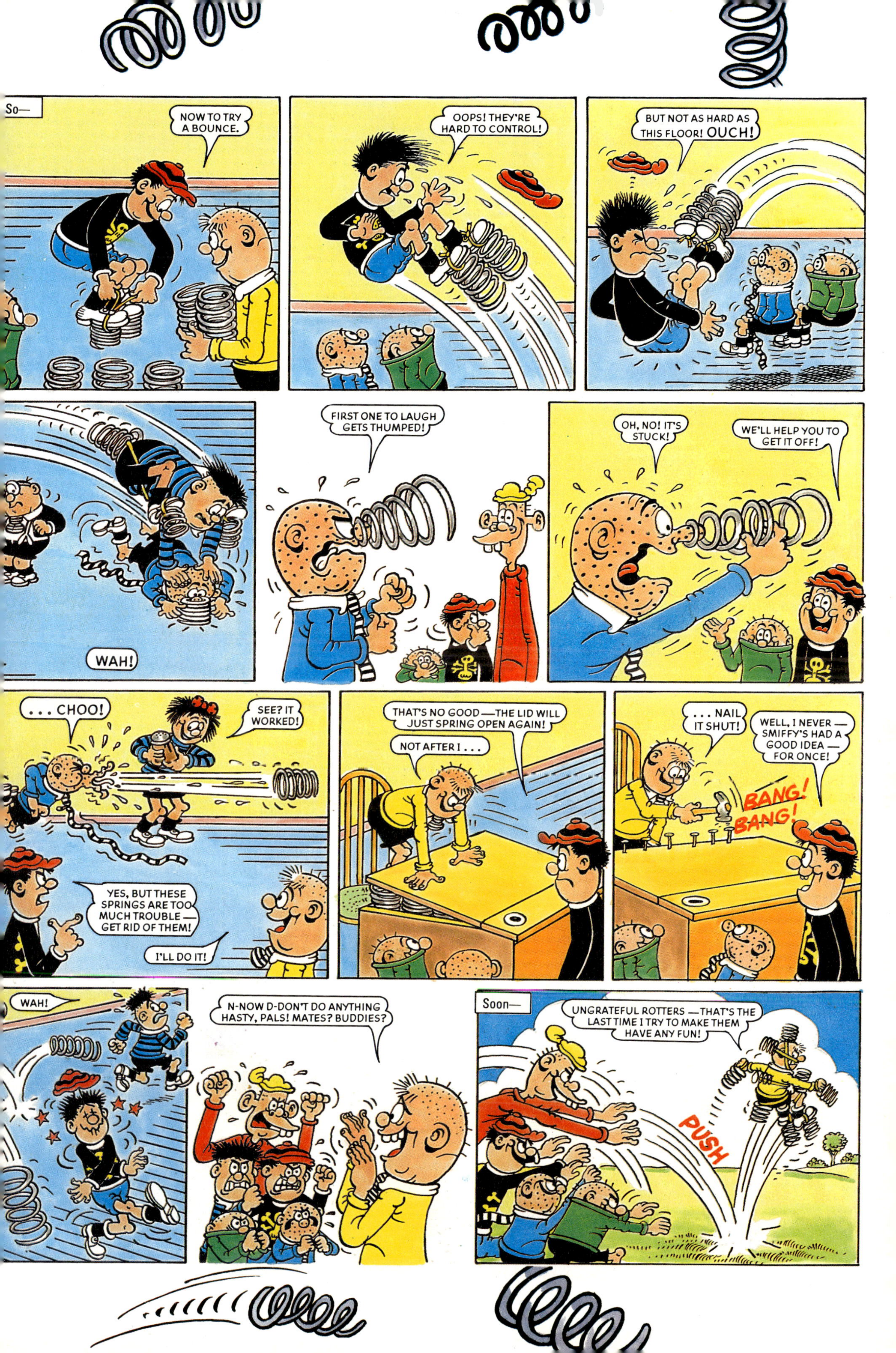
So—
NOW TO TRY A BOUNCE.
OOPS! THEY'RE HARD TO CONTROL!
BUT NOT AS HARD AS THIS FLOOR! OUCH!
WAH!
FIRST ONE TO LAUGH GETS THUMPED!
OH, NO! IT'S STUCK!
WE'LL HELP YOU TO GET IT OFF!
. . . CHOO!
SEE? IT WORKED!
YES, BUT THESE SPRINGS ARE TOO MUCH TROUBLE — GET RID OF THEM!
I'LL DO IT!
THAT'S NO GOOD — THE LID WILL JUST SPRING OPEN AGAIN!
NOT AFTER I . . .
. . . NAIL IT SHUT!
WELL, I NEVER — SMIFFY'S HAD A GOOD IDEA — FOR ONCE!
BANG! BANG!
WAH!
N-NOW D-DON'T DO ANYTHING HASTY, PALS! MATES? BUDDIES?
Soon—
UNGRATEFUL ROTTERS — THAT'S THE LAST TIME I TRY TO MAKE THEM HAVE ANY FUN!
PUSH

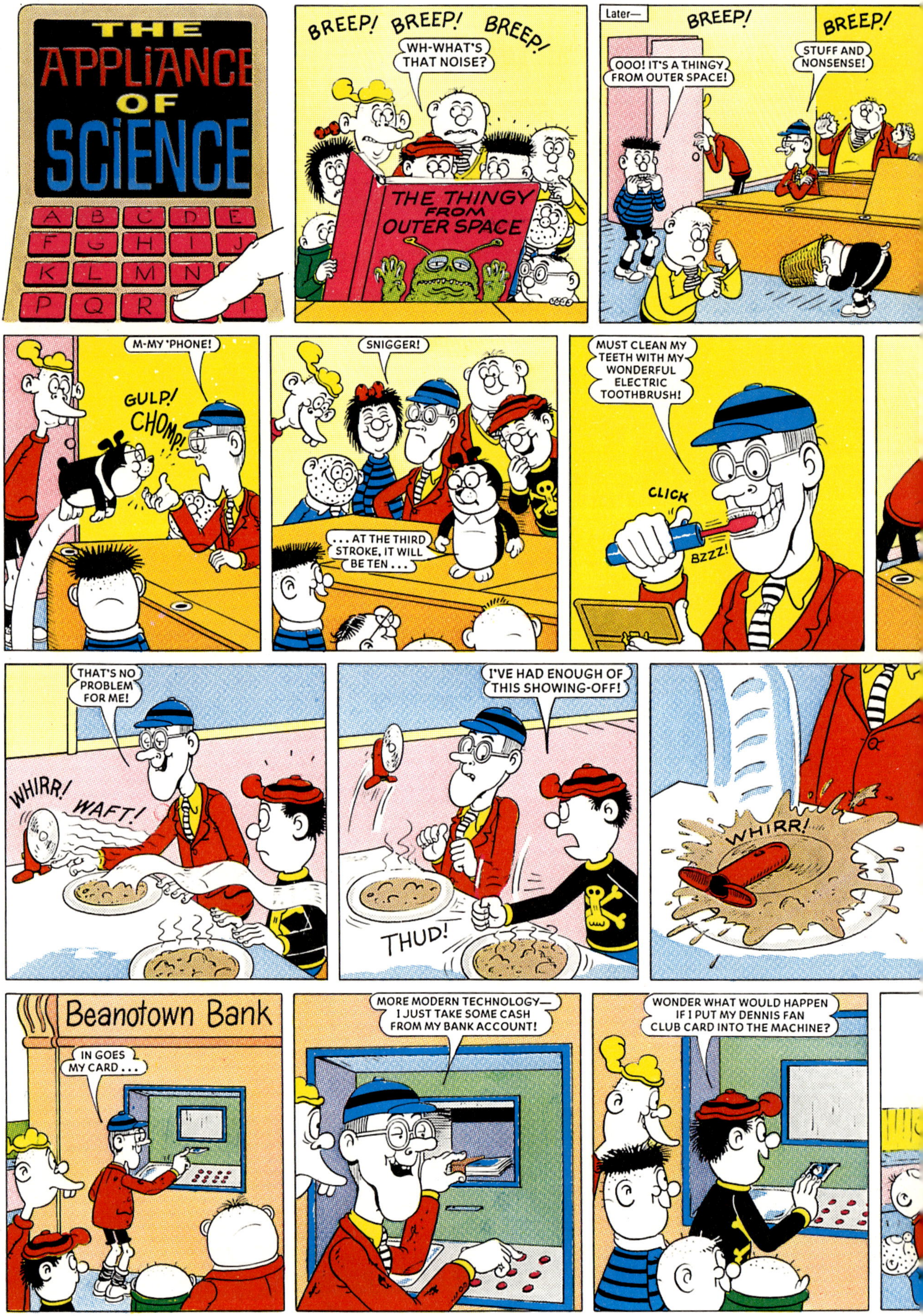
THE APPLIANCE OF SCIENCE
A B C D E
F G H I J
K L M N
P Q R
BREEP! BREEP! BREEP!
WH-WHAT'S THAT NOISE?
THE THINGY FROM OUTER SPACE
Later—
BREEP!
BREEP!
OOO! IT'S A THINGY FROM OUTER SPACE!
STUFF AND NONSENSE!
M-MY 'PHONE!
GULP!
CHOMP!
SNIGGER!
. . . AT THE THIRD STROKE, IT WILL BE TEN . . .
MUST CLEAN MY TEETH WITH MY WONDERFUL ELECTRIC TOOTHBRUSH!
CLICK
BZZZ!
THAT'S NO PROBLEM FOR ME!
WHIRR!
WAFT!
I'VE HAD ENOUGH OF THIS SHOWING-OFF!
THUD!
WHIRR!
Beanotown Bank
IN GOES MY CARD . . .
MORE MODERN TECHNOLOGY— I JUST TAKE SOME CASH FROM MY BANK ACCOUNT!
WONDER WHAT WOULD HAPPEN IF I PUT MY DENNIS FAN CLUB CARD INTO THE MACHINE?

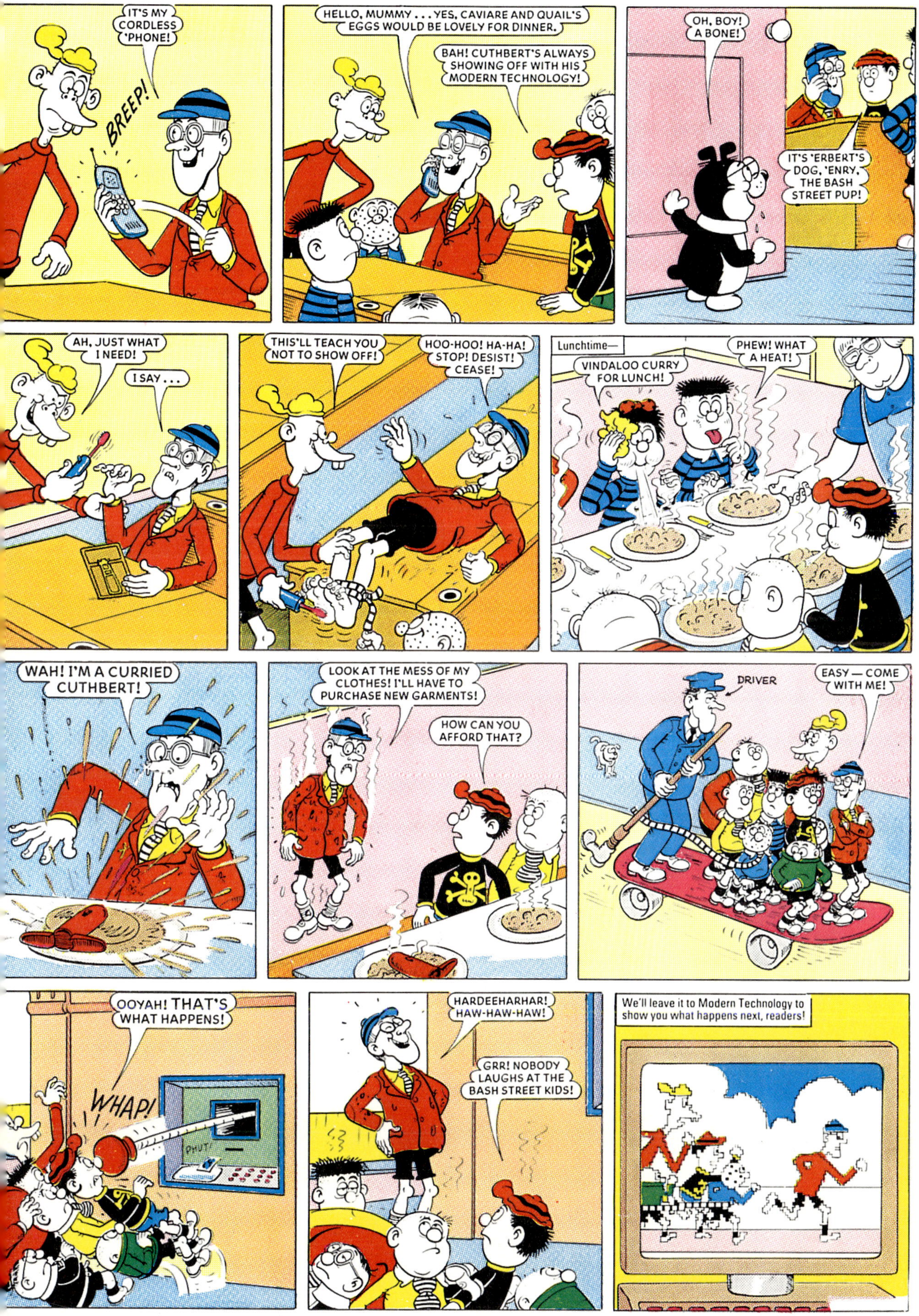
IT'S MY CORDLESS 'PHONE!
BREEP!
HELLO, MUMMY . . . YES, CAVIARE AND QUAIL'S EGGS WOULD BE LOVELY FOR DINNER.
BAH! CUTHBERT'S ALWAYS SHOWING OFF WITH HIS MODERN TECHNOLOGY!
OH, BOY! A BONE!
IT'S 'ERBERT'S DOG, 'ENRY, THE BASH STREET PUP!
AH, JUST WHAT I NEED!
I SAY . . .
THIS'LL TEACH YOU NOT TO SHOW OFF!
HOO-HOO! HA-HA! STOP! DESIST! CEASE!
Lunchtime—
VINDALOO CURRY FOR LUNCH!
PHEW! WHAT A HEAT!
WAH! I'M A CURRIED CUTHBERT!
LOOK AT THE MESS OF MY CLOTHES! I'LL HAVE TO PURCHASE NEW GARMENTS!
HOW CAN YOU AFFORD THAT?
DRIVER
EASY — COME WITH ME!
OOYAH! THAT'S WHAT HAPPENS!
WHAP!
PHUT!
HARDEEHARHAR! HAW-HAW-HAW!
GRR! NOBODY LAUGHS AT THE BASH STREET KIDS!
We'll leave it to Modern Technology to show you what happens next, readers!

FOR ART CLASS
SELF
THAT'S ME — FIVE MILES AWAY!
WELL, WE'RE TWINS — WE MUST LOOK LIKE THIS.
This is how 'Erbert sees himself!

LET'S TAKE A LOOK AT THE KIDS'
PORTRAITS
GOGH
TEACHER SAID ELF PORTRAIT, DIDN'T HE?
Modest as ever, Cuthbert!
Daft Smiffy forgot to put paper on his desk!
Close-up — VERY close-up!

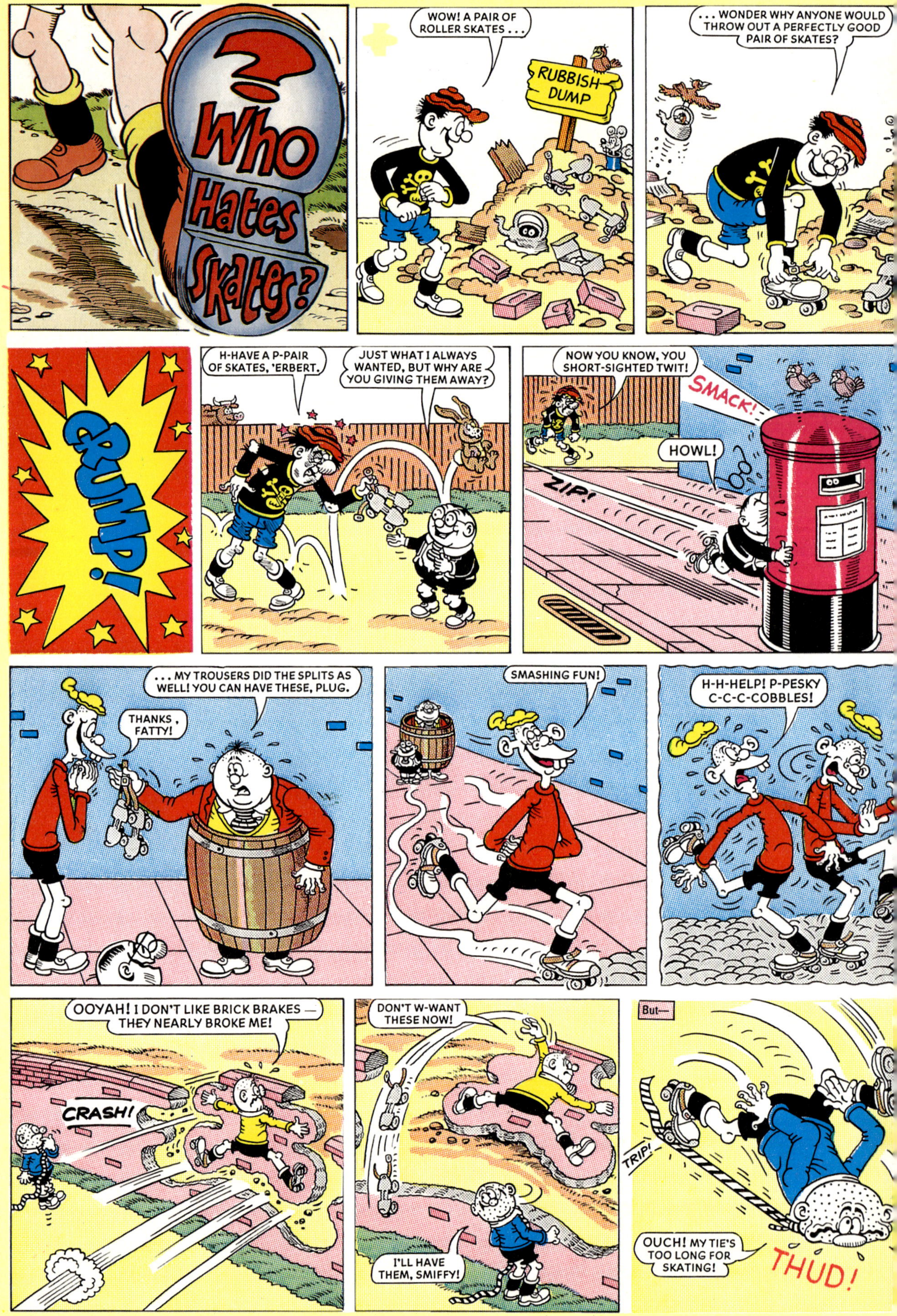
Who Hates Skates?
WOW! A PAIR OF ROLLER SKATES . . .
RUBBISH DUMP
. . . WONDER WHY ANYONE WOULD THROW OUT A PERFECTLY GOOD PAIR OF SKATES?
CRUMP!
H-HAVE A P-PAIR OF SKATES, 'ERBERT.
JUST WHAT I ALWAYS WANTED, BUT WHY ARE YOU GIVING THEM AWAY?
NOW YOU KNOW, YOU SHORT-SIGHTED TWIT!
SMACK!
HOWL!
ZIP!
. . . MY TROUSERS DID THE SPLITS AS WELL! YOU CAN HAVE THESE, PLUG.
THANKS, FATTY!
SMASHING FUN!
H-H-HELP! P-PESKY C-C-C-COBBLES!
OOYAH! I DON'T LIKE BRICK BRAKES — THEY NEARLY BROKE ME!
CRASH!
DON'T W-WANT THESE NOW!
I'LL HAVE THEM, SMIFFY!
But—
TRIP!
OUCH! MY TIE'S TOO LONG FOR SKATING!
THUD!

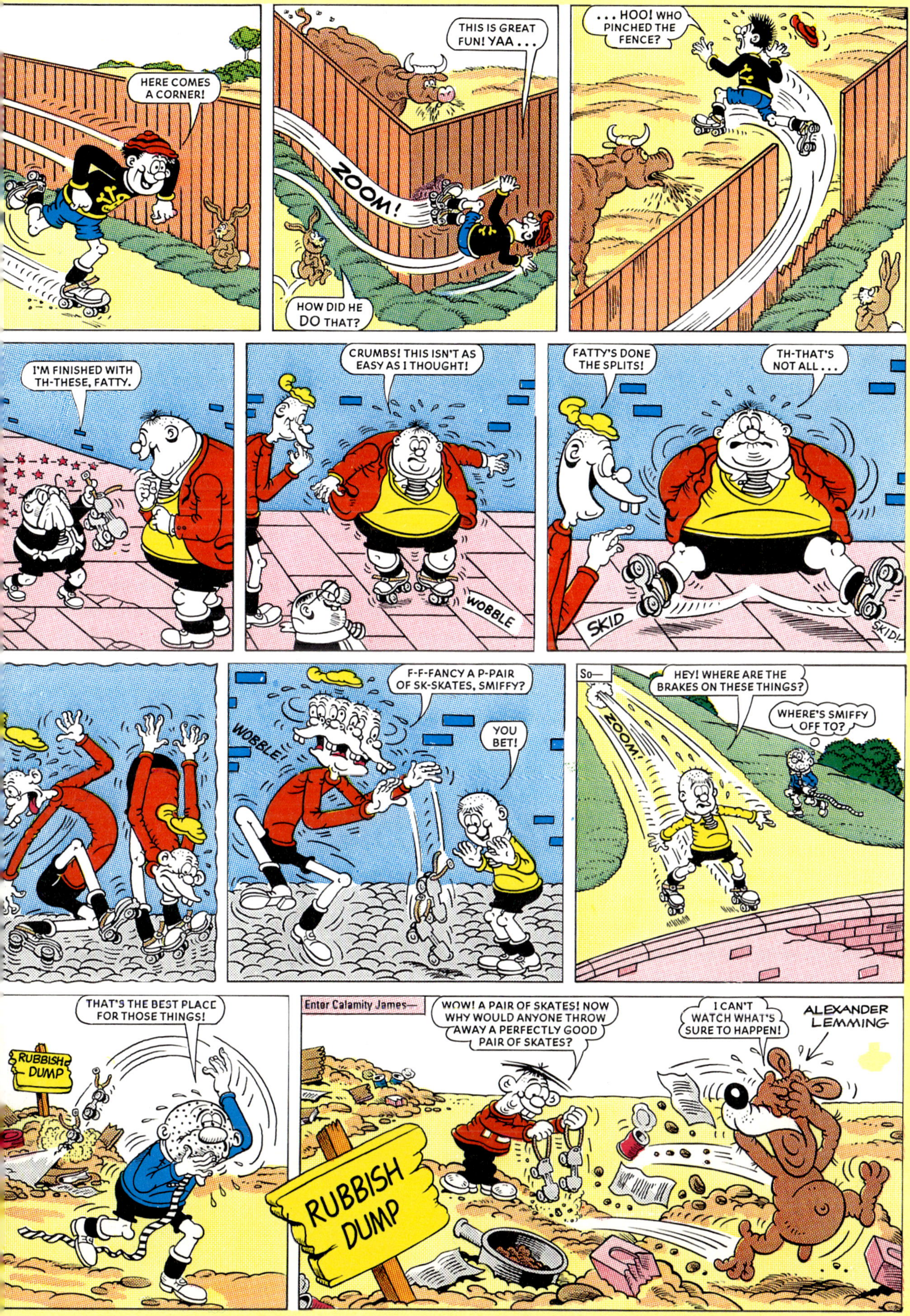
HERE COMES A CORNER!
THIS IS GREAT FUN! YAA . . .
ZOOM!
HOW DID HE DO THAT?
. . . HOO! WHO PINCHED THE FENCE?
I'M FINISHED WITH TH-THESE, FATTY.
CRUMBS! THIS ISN'T AS EASY AS I THOUGHT!
WOBBLE
FATTY'S DONE THE SPLITS!
TH-THAT'S NOT ALL . . .
SKID
SKID!
WOBBLE!
F-F-FANCY A P-PAIR OF SK-SKATES, SMIFFY?
YOU BET!
So—
HEY! WHERE ARE THE BRAKES ON THESE THINGS?
WHERE'S SMIFFY OFF TO?
ZOOM!
THAT'S THE BEST PLACE FOR THOSE THINGS!
RUBBISH DUMP
Enter Calamity James—
WOW! A PAIR OF SKATES! NOW WHY WOULD ANYONE THROW AWAY A PERFECTLY GOOD PAIR OF SKATES?
I CAN'T WATCH WHAT'S SURE TO HAPPEN!
ALEXANDER LEMMING
RUBBISH DUMP

Put the Boot in!

WITH THE BASH STREET PUPS

NECKS PLEASE
Which of the following uses for Spotty's tie do YOU think is best? Answer at the foot of the page.
SPIN IT ROUND TO COOL YOU ON A HOT DAY.
LOVELY BREEZE
SPIN IT HARDER AND YOU CAN GO ON A SHORT FLIGHT.
WHIRR
SPOTTY'S HOME WORK
LIFT
IT'S A HANDY TAPE MEASURE.
COO! SNITCHY MCPHEE'S HOOTER'S 10 CMS LONG!
AS A WHIP TO KEEP BACK FIERCE ANIMALS.
CRACK!
SNARL! FINISHED THE LAST OF MY MILK HE DID.
A SKIPPING ROPE.
WHIRR!
BOING
BOING
A LEAD.
ANSWER! THEY'RE ALL EQUALLY GOOD USES . . . IT'S A TIE!

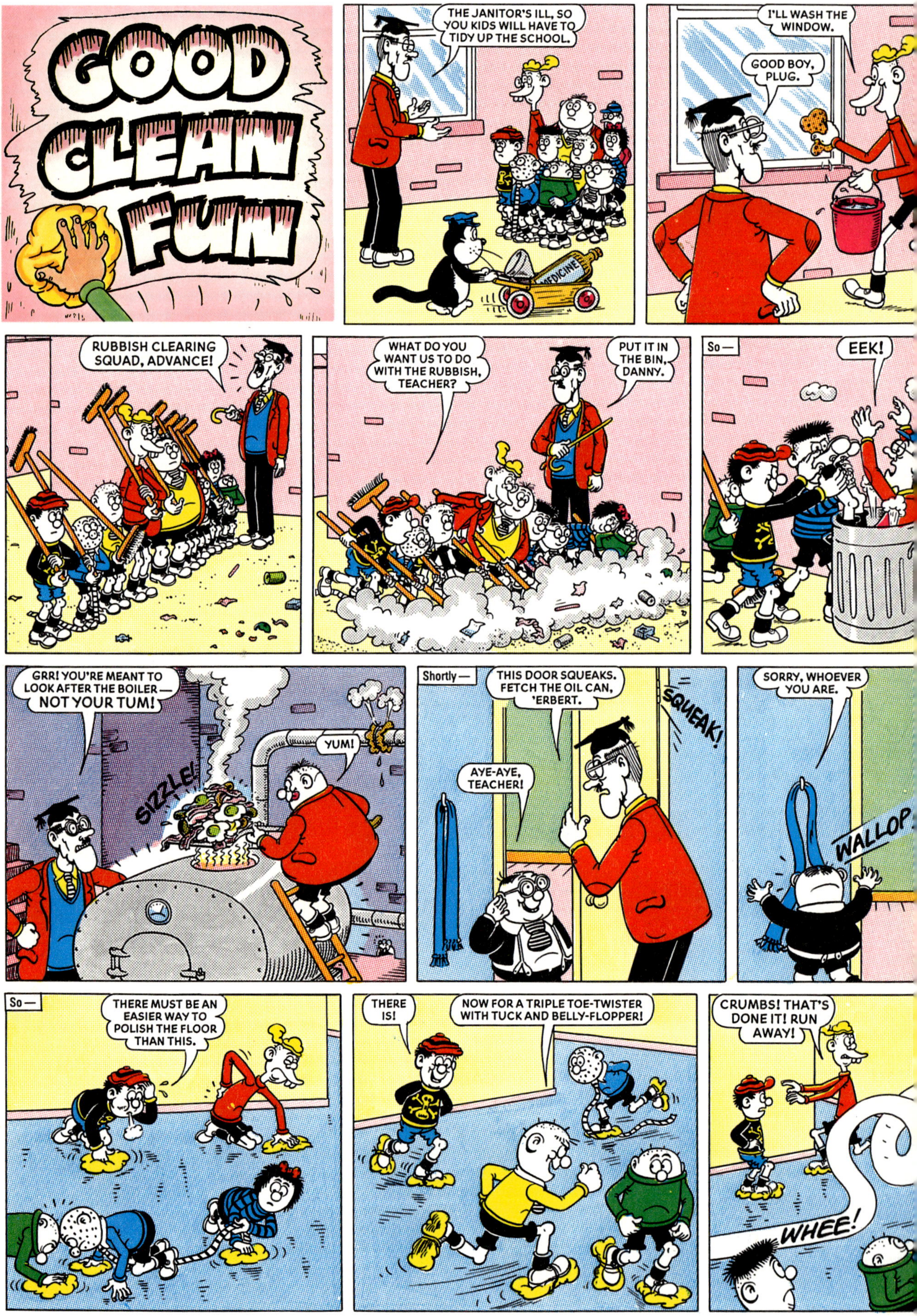
GOOD CLEAN FUN
THE JANITOR'S ILL, SO YOU KIDS WILL HAVE TO TIDY UP THE SCHOOL.
I'LL WASH THE WINDOW.
GOOD BOY, PLUG.
RUBBISH CLEARING SQUAD, ADVANCE!
WHAT DO YOU WANT US TO DO WITH THE RUBBISH, TEACHER?
PUT IT IN THE BIN, DANNY.
So—
EEK!
GRR! YOU'RE MEANT TO LOOK AFTER THE BOILER — NOT YOUR TUM!
YUM!
SIZZLE!
Shortly—
THIS DOOR SQUEAKS. FETCH THE OIL CAN, 'ERBERT.
SQUEAK!
AYE-AYE, TEACHER!
SORRY, WHOEVER YOU ARE.
WALLOP!
So—
THERE MUST BE AN EASIER WAY TO POLISH THE FLOOR THAN THIS.
THERE IS!
NOW FOR A TRIPLE TOE-TWISTER WITH TUCK AND BELLY-FLOPPER!
CRUMBS! THAT'S DONE IT! RUN AWAY!
WHEE!

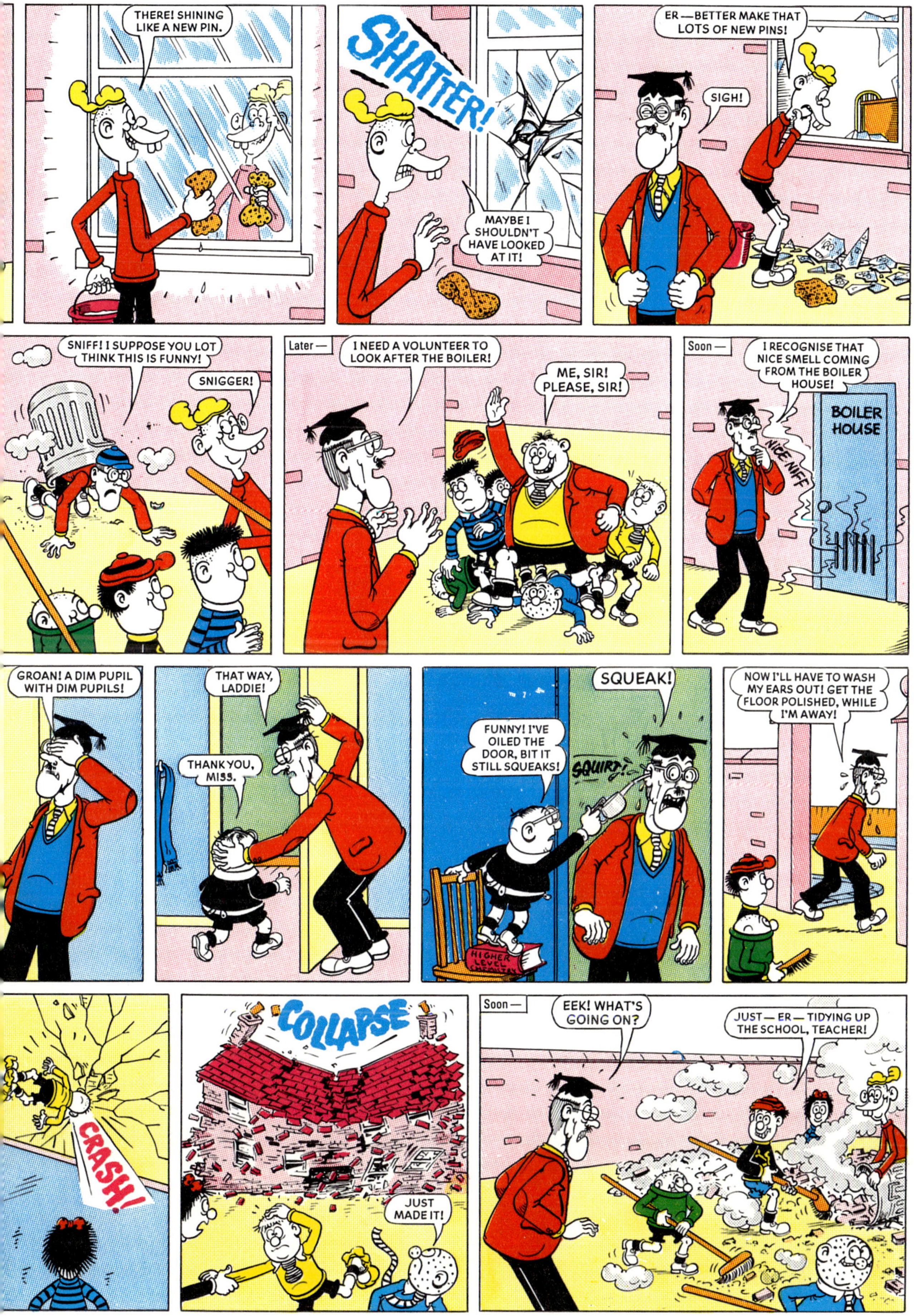
THERE! SHINING LIKE A NEW PIN.
SHATTER!
MAYBE I SHOULDN'T HAVE LOOKED AT IT!
ER — BETTER MAKE THAT LOTS OF NEW PINS!
SIGH!
SNIFF! I SUPPOSE YOU LOT THINK THIS IS FUNNY!
SNIGGER!
Later —
I NEED A VOLUNTEER TO LOOK AFTER THE BOILER!
ME, SIR! PLEASE, SIR!
Soon —
I RECOGNISE THAT NICE SMELL COMING FROM THE BOILER HOUSE!
BOILER HOUSE
NICE NIFF
GROAN! A DIM PUPIL WITH DIM PUPILS!
THAT WAY, LADDIE!
THANK YOU, MISS.
SQUEAK!
FUNNY! I'VE OILED THE DOOR, BIT IT STILL SQUEAKS!
SQUIRT!
HIGHER LEVEL
NOW I'LL HAVE TO WASH MY EARS OUT! GET THE FLOOR POLISHED, WHILE I'M AWAY!
CRASH!
COLLAPSE
JUST MADE IT!
Soon —
EEK! WHAT'S GOING ON?
JUST — ER — TIDYING UP THE SCHOOL, TEACHER!

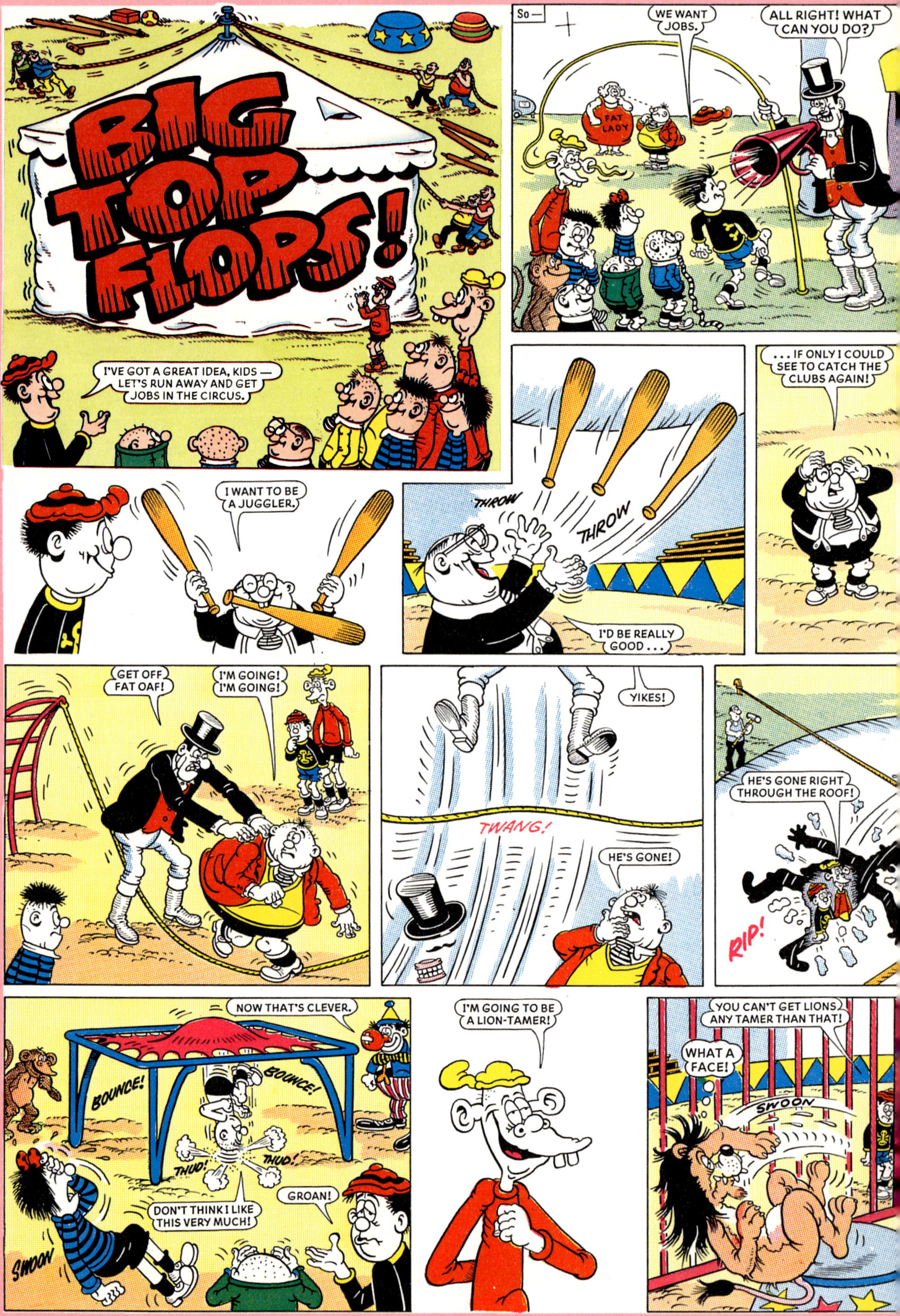
BIG TOP FLOPS!
I'VE GOT A GREAT IDEA, KIDS — LET'S RUN AWAY AND GET JOBS IN THE CIRCUS.
So—
WE WANT JOBS.
ALL RIGHT! WHAT CAN YOU DO?
FAT LADY
I WANT TO BE A JUGGLER.
THROW
THROW
I'D BE REALLY GOOD . . .
. . . IF ONLY I COULD SEE TO CATCH THE CLUBS AGAIN!
GET OFF FAT OAF!
I'M GOING! I'M GOING!
YIKES!
TWANG!
HE'S GONE!
HE'S GONE RIGHT THROUGH THE ROOF!
RIP!
NOW THAT'S CLEVER.
BOUNCE!
BOUNCE!
THUD!
THUD!
DON'T THINK I LIKE THIS VERY MUCH!
GROAN!
SWOON
I'M GOING TO BE A LION-TAMER!
YOU CAN'T GET LIONS ANY TAMER THAN THAT!
WHAT A FACE!
SWOON

YOU COULD BE A TRAPEZE ARTIST, CUTHBERT! UP, YOU GO!
MUST I?
G-GET M-ME D-DOWN! I'M SC-SCARED OF H-HEIGHTS!
WHAT A WIMP!
HUH! IF THAT "HEIGHT" WAS ANY CLOSER TO THE GROUND, IT WOULD BE A LOW!
WHINE!
DUH-H!
I FANCY BEING THE TIGHTROPE WALKER.
LEAP
AHEM! MAYBE I'M JUST A BIT HEAVY FOR THIS!
CLUNK!
WHEE!
WHIMPER! GET M-ME D-DOWN!
Meanwhile —
WHAT ARE YOU DOING, SMIFFY?
TUG
I'M GOING TO BE A BARE-BACK RIDER!
THAT MEANS THE HORSE IS BARE-BACKED — NOT YOU, YOU TWIT!
OK! IN THAT CASE, I'LL BE THE DARING YOUNG BOY ON THE SPRINGY THINGY!
TRAMPOLINE
COOEE!
SWOON
WELL, WHAT CAN WE DO, MISTER?
I DON'T KNOW ABOUT YOU, BUT I KNOW WHAT WE'RE GOING TO DO . . .
CIRCUS
VAROOOM!
HUH! THE CIRCUS HAS RUN AWAY TO WORK ANY PLACE OTHER THAN HERE!

WHOSE CREST IS BEST?
On the way to school—
OBSERVE MY SMART PUPILS IN THEIR STYLISH BLAZERS, OLD CHAP!
I DESIGNED THE CREST MYSELF, YOU KNOW.
Blob Street Teacher
SMARTUS ALEXUS
VERY NICE, I'M SURE.
Bash Street Teacher
SHLURP! IT'S A DEAL!
GRAB!
So—
I COULDN'T AFFORD A BLAZER EACH — SO THIS IS THE NEXT BEST THING!
PHUT!
FASTEN
WHAT CREST IS THAT, FATTY?
AND HERE'S THE RESULT!
BASHSTREETKIDS
WAIT A MINUTE — WE CAN'T SEW THE CREST — NO SEWING MACHINE!
I'LL GET HELP, TEACHER.
GNIPPER WILL DO NICELY.
GNIP! GNIP!
AH, TOOTS HAS SEWN THE CREST ON BEAUTIFULLY.
TIME TO GO HOME, TEACHER!
RING!
VERY SMART!
BASH ST SCHOOL
BASH ST SCHOOL
SEE YOU!
SEE YOU TOMORROW!

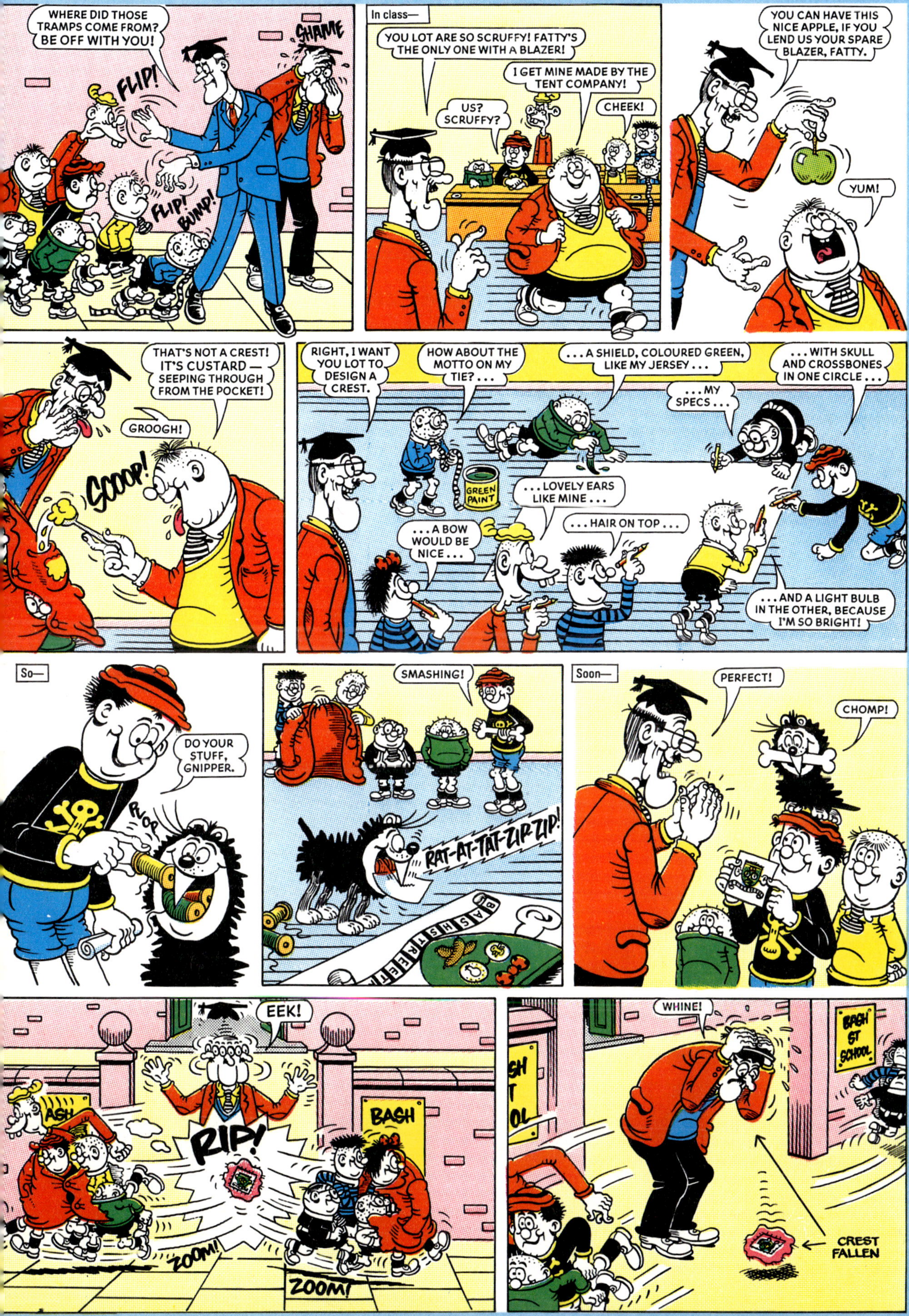
WHERE DID THOSE TRAMPS COME FROM? BE OFF WITH YOU!
SHAME
FLIP!
FLIP!
BUMP!
In class—
YOU LOT ARE SO SCRUFFY! FATTY'S THE ONLY ONE WITH A BLAZER!
I GET MINE MADE BY THE TENT COMPANY!
US? SCRUFFY?
CHEEK!
YOU CAN HAVE THIS NICE APPLE, IF YOU LEND US YOUR SPARE BLAZER, FATTY.
YUM!
THAT'S NOT A CREST! IT'S CUSTARD — SEEPING THROUGH FROM THE POCKET!
GROOGH!
SQOOP!
RIGHT, I WANT YOU LOT TO DESIGN A CREST.
HOW ABOUT THE MOTTO ON MY TIE? . . .
. . . A SHIELD, COLOURED GREEN, LIKE MY JERSEY . . .
. . . WITH SKULL AND CROSSBONES IN ONE CIRCLE . . .
. . . MY SPECS . . .
GREEN PAINT
. . . LOVELY EARS LIKE MINE . . .
. . . A BOW WOULD BE NICE . . .
. . . HAIR ON TOP . . .
. . . AND A LIGHT BULB IN THE OTHER, BECAUSE I'M SO BRIGHT!
So—
DO YOUR STUFF, GNIPPER.
PLOP
SMASHING!
RAT-AT-TAT-ZIP-ZIP!
BASH STREET
Soon—
PERFECT!
CHOMP!
EEK!
BASH
RIP!
BASH
ZOOM!
ZOOM!
WHINE!
BASH ST SCHOOL
CREST FALLEN

MODEL PUPILS
OL
WHAT'S THE DIFFERENCE BETWEEN A COYOTE AND A FLEA?
ONE HOWLS ON THE PRAIRIE AND THE OTHER PROWLS ON THE HAIRY!
WHO BURPED AT THE BIG BAD WOLF?
LITTLE RUDE RIDING HOOD!
NAME TWO DAYS BEGINNING WITH 'T'!
ER — TODAY AND TOMORROW!

WHAT BIRD STEALS CUTLERY? A FORK LIFT DUCK!
WHAT'S BLACK AND WHITE AND FOUND IN AFRICA?
A ZEBRA?
NO — A PENGUIN ON HOLIDAY!
WHAT DO YOU CALL A SECRET AGENT WHO LIVES IN A WASHING UP BOTTLE?
BUBBLE O SEVEN!
These models are now available in all leading giftware shops.

LET'S PRETEND
I'M FED UP OF JUST BEING A BASH STREET KID, PALS — LET'S BE SOMETHING ELSE!
So—
WE'RE BEING AEROPLANES!
Birdbrain.
BACK, BACK I SAY!
MY SHOULDERS ARE BACK!
NOW WE'RE BEING AN AVALANCHE!
CRUMP!
S-SOMEBODY G-GET THE N-NUMBER OF THAT ELEPHANT!
D-DON'T FEEL LIKE EATING NOW.
YOUR FISH, SIR.
N-NO, TA!
GOOD FUN, THAT! WHAT CAN WE BE THIS TIME?
LET'S BE . . .
. . . DOGGIES — ROWF!
Later—
IT'S ONLY TAKEN FOUR HOURS, BUT I'VE FINALLY MANAGED TO . . .
. . . START A FIRE BY RUBBING TWO STICKS TOGETHER.
WE'RE BEING FIREMEN NOW!

OOPS!
YIPE!
Meanwhile—
KEEP THOSE SHOULDERS BACK, LOVELY BOYS— VERY, VERY SMART.
TOOT!
Soon—
FISH & CHIPS
I'VE GOT A GREAT IDEA — LET'S BE . . .
GOLDFISH!
MEEOW!
OH, NO — SOUNDS LIKE GNASHER, GNIPPER, THE BASH STREET PUPS AND THE HOUND OF THE BASKETBALLS!
YAP!
GRR!
GROWL!
P.O.
GRR! IT WAS THOSE PESKY KIDS!
YAP!
SNAP!
WHIMPER!
OUCH!
WAH!
GUESS WHAT WE'RE BEING NOW, READERS — THAT'S RIGHT — WE'RE BEING . . .
. . . CHASED FOR OUR LIVES!

WHAT'S THE USE?
YOU'RE A BUNCH OF USELESS, DIM-WITTED, DISGUSTING, STUPID PUPILS!
HOMEWORK
WE OBJECT TO THAT!
. . . TO PROVE I'M USEFUL AT GETTING RID OF FLIES!
AND MORTAR BOARDS — MINE'S STUCK UP THERE!
I'M USEFUL TOO! MY EARS MAKE GREAT SUCTION CUPS TO HELP ME CLIMB UP TO GET YOUR HAT BACK!
SMACK!
WELL, I NEVER . . .
THERE YOU ARE.
NOW I'M SOAKED!
NOT FOR LONG— FATTY WILL BE USEFUL NOW!
CURRY
SHEEEESH!
HOT
BLAST!
MY CLOTHES— THEY'RE ALL SINGED AND RUINED!
YES, BUT THEY'RE DRY!
I LOOK LIKE A COMPLETE IDIOT!
NO, YOU DON'T . . .
. . . TO LOOK LIKE A COMPLETE IDIOT, YOU'LL HAVE TO WEAR THIS!
SEE? EVEN SMIFFY'S USEFUL! HE KNOWS ALL ABOUT IDIOTS!
MY GOODNESS!

WE'RE NOT USELESS AND WE'LL PROVE IT!
OH, YES?
HOMEWORK FOR DOLTS
BAH! A PESKY FLY!
WALL CHART
THIS IS MY CHANCE...
YIKE!
CRACK!
WAH! I'M FILTHY!
WE'RE USEFUL FOR MAKING YOU CLEAN AGAIN!
GLUBBLE!
SQUIRT!
I CAN BE USEFUL NOW — I PICKED UP MUM'S WASHING INSTEAD OF MY SCHOOLBAG, THIS MORNING!
THIS WILL REPLACE YOUR RUINED CLOTHES, TEACHER!
THE POOR MAN — HE'S FINALLY FLIPPED!
TAKE THE DAY OFF! I'LL LOOK AFTER YOUR CLASS, OLD CHAP!
IIB
At home—
THE KIDS WERE RIGHT— THEY ARE USEFUL!

SAFETY FIRST-TEACHER LAST!
TODAY I'M GOING TO TEACH YOU ABOUT ROAD SAFETY. NOW YOU MAY THINK ROADS ARE SAFE . . .
. . . AFTER ALL — WHO COULD HURT A ROAD? TITTER! JUST A LITTLE JOKE!
TRIP!
BUMPER HOLS 85
Suddenly —
WAA!
THUD!
WHOOSH!
NOT THE BEST POSITION THERE TEACHER, OUTSIDE BILLY WHIZZ'S HOUSE WHEN HE'S LATE FOR SCHOOL!
SHAKE
WHIZZ!
OOF!
SPLAT!
GNASH! SNORT! GNIP!
EEK!
. . . TOO LATE!
HELP! WAA!
NEVER TAKE A SHORTCUT . . .
. . . THROUGH DENNIS'S GARDEN!
NOT WHEN GNASHER, GNIPPER AND RASHER ARE THERE! PHEW!
YEAAARGH!
THAT'S AN ODD THING TO BE SAYING!
ZOOM!
PYOING!
WHEE!
OH, NO! I'M GOING TO LAND IN . . .

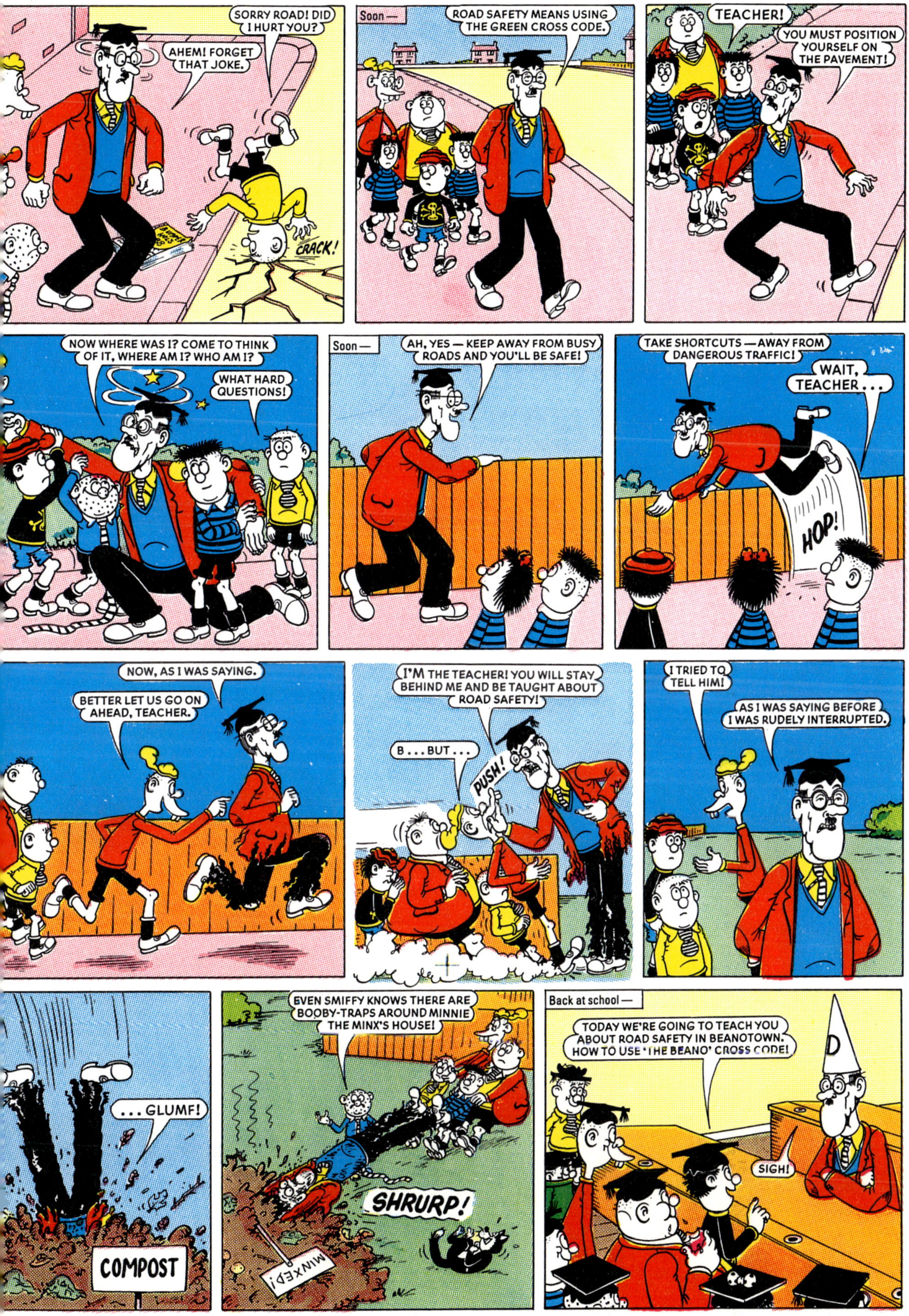

SORRY ROAD! DID I HURT YOU?
AHEM! FORGET THAT JOKE.
CRACK!
Soon —
ROAD SAFETY MEANS USING THE GREEN CROSS CODE.
TEACHER!
YOU MUST POSITION YOURSELF ON THE PAVEMENT!
NOW WHERE WAS I? COME TO THINK OF IT, WHERE AM I? WHO AM I?
WHAT HARD QUESTIONS!
Soon —
AH, YES — KEEP AWAY FROM BUSY ROADS AND YOU'LL BE SAFE!
TAKE SHORTCUTS — AWAY FROM DANGEROUS TRAFFIC!
WAIT, TEACHER . . .
HOP!
NOW, AS I WAS SAYING.
BETTER LET US GO ON AHEAD, TEACHER.
I'M THE TEACHER! YOU WILL STAY BEHIND ME AND BE TAUGHT ABOUT ROAD SAFETY!
B . . . BUT . . .
PUSH!
I TRIED TO TELL HIM!
AS I WAS SAYING BEFORE I WAS RUDELY INTERRUPTED.
. . . GLUMF!
COMPOST
EVEN SMIFFY KNOWS THERE ARE BOOBY-TRAPS AROUND MINNIE THE MINX'S HOUSE!
SHRURP!
MINXED!
Back at school —
TODAY WE'RE GOING TO TEACH YOU ABOUT ROAD SAFETY IN BEANOTOWN. HOW TO USE 'THE BEANO' CROSS CODE!
D
SIGH!

CRAZY PAVING
The BASH STREET PUPS
WOW! They've been laying new paving slabs in our street.
Very nice!
Even under our bin? Er— thank you!
There's something wrong here, but what is it?
It's our buried bones - we can't get at them!
Pesky paving slabs!
Sob! Our precious bones!
RUMBLE!
Erk! We've started an earthquake!
WOOMFF!
Wah!
I've been tunnelling, pals! Hey what are YOU doing in Australia?
Good old daft Sniffy!
I must have taken a wrong turn at Greece.
BONES
SNIFFY
WIGGY
PUG
TUSSY
MANFRID
PEEPS
BLOTTY

Winston's KRAZY KATTERY

Hysterical History
. . . AND THE ROUNDHEADS FOUGHT THE CAVALIERS DURING THE ENGLISH CIVIL WAR.
I'VE ALWAYS WISHED I COULD HAVE BEEN A CAVALIER.
JAB!
AH! BEING CHIVALROUS TO GOOD QUEEN BESS, YOU MEAN?
E.R. RULES
DRY CLEAN ONLY
NO . . .
TIP
THERMOS CASK
I WOULD LOVE TO HAVE BEEN BONNIE PRINCE CHARLIE!
CULLODEN
A96
RUN AWAY, CHAPS! LOOK AT THAT UGLY FACE!
HOOTS!
IF YOU HAD BEEN, IT COULD HAVE CHANGED THE COURSE OF HISTORY!
I WOULD LOVE TO HAVE BEEN DICK TURPIN!
FASTER, BESS — THEY BE GAINING ON US!
WOOF! WOOF!
Suddenly —
WAA!
CRASH!
OW!
OO . . . ER! WHAT WILL THE JANITOR SAY?

YOU MEAN YOU'D LIKE TO BE A CAR?
ONE VERY DIM PUPIL
NOT A VAUXHALL CAVALIER, YOU BRAINLESS BUFFOON!
IF I COULD BE ANYONE IN HISTORY IT WOULD BE SIR WALTER RALEIGH.
... DISCOVERING THE POTATO! YUM!
HEAT
VERY COSY
I'D HAVE LIKED TO HAVE BEEN QUEEN BOADECIA, FIGHTING THE ROMANS!
GASP! IF I COULD BE ANYONE IN HISTORY — IT WOULDN'T BE QUEEN BOADECIA'S HORSE!
AND I'D HAVE BEEN BLACK BESS, HIS HORSE.
SOOT
WHUMF!
HOI! TAKING OUR BEANOS IS HIGHWAY ROBBERY!
GRAB
BEANO
THANK YE! HAR-HAR!
FATTY'S LUNCH
MOO! MOO!
I'D SAY — YAHOO!
EH?
JUMP
MY HERO IN HISTORY WAS THAT GREAT BUILDER OF WALLS — EMPEROR HADRIAN!

SPOUSE GROUSE
WE CAN'T WAIT TO GET TO SCHOOL TODAY . . .
. . . TEACHER'S NOT WELL!
SO IT'S GOING TO BE AN EASY DAY FOR US!
AHCHOO!
. . . THIS IS MRS TEACHER!
EH?
HELLO, CHILDREN! I HAVEN'T TAUGHT SINCE I GOT MARRIED, BUT I'M SURE WE'LL GET ALONG JUST FINE.
IF THEY CAUSE ANY TROUBLE, JUST RING!
THANK YOU.
SIT DOWN, YOU LOT!
SHEESH!
HMM! LOTS OF EXTRA HOMEWORK IN HERE. YOURS, ISN'T IT, CUTHBERT?
NO!
THAT'S MINE! I WONDERED WHERE MY PLAYTIME SNACK HAD GONE!
UGH!
WHAT'S THIS TABLECLOTH HERE FOR?
SNIGGER! MY PLAN'S PUT INTO ACTION.
THAT SOUND . . .
. . I FORGOT! MUST DASH, PUPILS!
IT WORKED! SHE JUST COULDN'T MISS . . .

So —
THIS IS GREAT FUN!
Meanwhile —
SORRY TO HEAR TEACHER'S ILL. NOW WE'VE NOBODY TO TAKE HIS CLASS.
HMM!
Soon —
AHEM! HERE IS YOUR REPLACEMENT TEACHER FOR TODAY . . .
LOUD
DIN!
GASP!
WOW!
GET THIS PLACE CLEANED UP AT ONCE!
YES, SIR! I MEAN, MRS!
SMIFFY ISN'T 'ALF HERE
ARE YOU GOING TO HELP US?
NO, I NEED THESE GLOVES TO PROTECT MY HANDS WHILE I INSPECT YOUR HOMEWORK BOOKS!
THAT'S MINE! I MISSED MY JOTTER!
HOPELESS, USELESS AND HORRID! WE'LL DO VERY, VERY HARD SUMS!
GOODY!
BADDY!
I HAVE A PLAN.
. . . ONCE A JOLLY DINGO . . .
. . . "KANGAROO STREET", THE AUSTRALIAN SOAP!
OH, WILL BRUCE BEACHBOY MARRY SHEILA SHEEPDIP?
THAT'LL KEEP MRS T. OUT OF OUR WAY FOR AN HOUR!

CHECK IT OUT!
POSHE ACADEMY KIDS APPROACHING.
LET'S GET THEM!
BASH STREET SCHOOL
Back at school —
HAVEN'T USED THIS FOR SOME TIME!
CHESS SET
FROM OLIVE
HIGHER MATHS
LOWER MATHS
HALLEY'S COMET
ERK! THE WOODWORMS HAVE EATEN ALL THE PIECES.
WE'LL DRESS UP AS CHESS PIECES AND SEE YOU AT THE GIANT CHESSBOARD AT THE PARK!
CHEESE SET
WE'RE CASTLES!
THEY'RE BISHOPS.
BUT I'M THE ONLY PAWN. WE NEED SEVEN MORE.
HMM.
I SAY! SUCH SCRUFFS! OUR TAILOR-MADE OUTFITS ARE MUCH NICER THAN YOURS.
WHO ARE YOU CALLING SCRUFFS?
FOUL! YOU'RE NOT ALLOWED TO MOVE LIKE THAT!

OH, NO!
SCRAP
CEASE THIS UNRULY BEHAVIOUR, RUFFIANS!
ERK!
WE PREFER BRAINS TO BRAWN! WE CHALLENGE YOU TO A CHESS MATCH!
W-WE CAN'T TURN DOWN A CHALLENGE!
OK! WE'LL MEET YOU THERE AT HIGH NOON!
WE'LL BE KING AND QUEEN!
WE'RE THE KNIGHTS!
I CAN FIX THAT.
SCHOOL OFFICE
LIE STILL.
PHOTO-COPYING MACHINE
FILES
Soon—
STICK THESE ON TO BOARDS AND WE'LL HAVE AS MANY PAWNS AS WE NEED.
BZZZZ!
So—
SMIFFY
HOWL!
BOP!
WHACK!
CHECKMATE, I THINK!
SIGH!

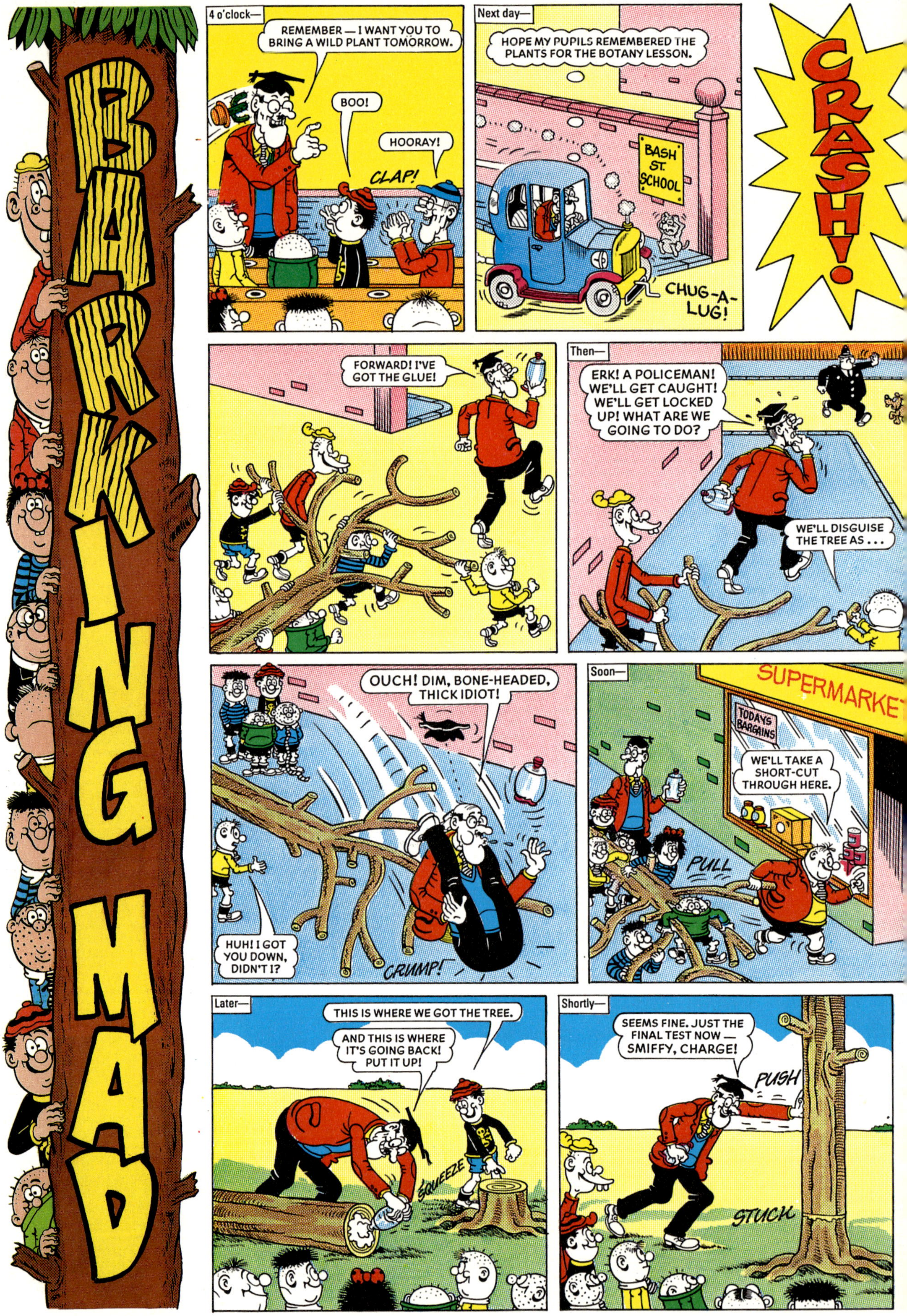
BARKING MAD
4 o'clock—
REMEMBER — I WANT YOU TO BRING A WILD PLANT TOMORROW.
BOO!
HOORAY!
CLAP!
Next day—
HOPE MY PUPILS REMEMBERED THE PLANTS FOR THE BOTANY LESSON.
BASH ST. SCHOOL
CHUG-A-LUG!
CRASH!
FORWARD! I'VE GOT THE GLUE!
Then—
ERK! A POLICEMAN! WE'LL GET CAUGHT! WE'LL GET LOCKED UP! WHAT ARE WE GOING TO DO?
WE'LL DISGUISE THE TREE AS . . .
OUCH! DIM, BONE-HEADED, THICK IDIOT!
HUH! I GOT YOU DOWN, DIDN'T I?
CRUMP!
Soon—
SUPERMARKET
TODAYS BARGAINS
WE'LL TAKE A SHORT-CUT THROUGH HERE.
PULL
Later—
THIS IS WHERE WE GOT THE TREE.
AND THIS IS WHERE IT'S GOING BACK! PUT IT UP!
SQUEEZE
Shortly—
SEEMS FINE. JUST THE FINAL TEST NOW — SMIFFY, CHARGE!
PUSH
STUCK

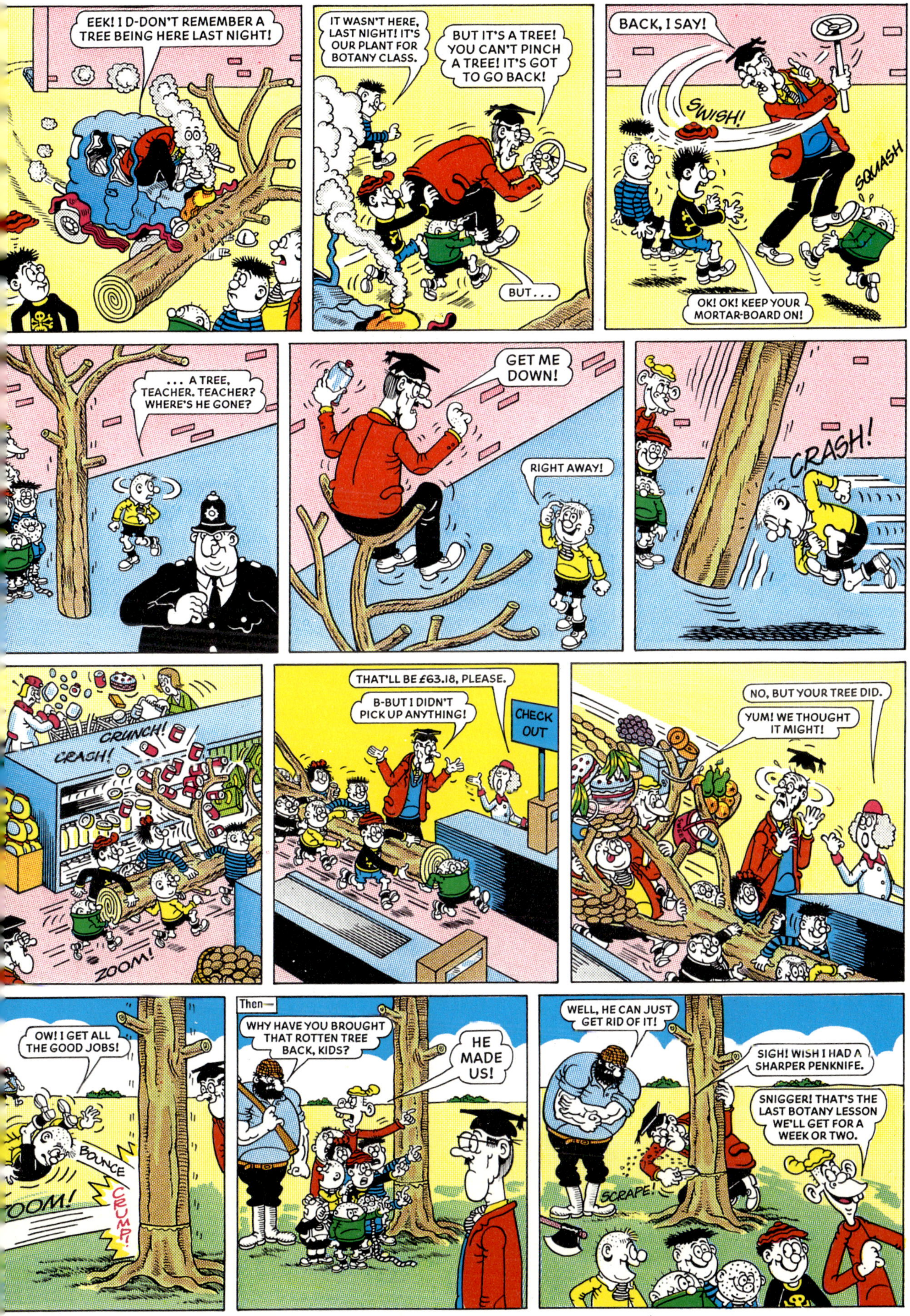

EEK! I D-DON'T REMEMBER A TREE BEING HERE LAST NIGHT!
IT WASN'T HERE, LAST NIGHT! IT'S OUR PLANT FOR BOTANY CLASS.
BUT IT'S A TREE! YOU CAN'T PINCH A TREE! IT'S GOT TO GO BACK!
BUT . . .
BACK, I SAY!
SWISH!
SQUASH
OK! OK! KEEP YOUR MORTAR-BOARD ON!
. . . A TREE, TEACHER. TEACHER? WHERE'S HE GONE?
GET ME DOWN!
RIGHT AWAY!
CRASH!
CRUNCH!
CRASH!
ZOOM!
THAT'LL BE £63.18, PLEASE.
B-BUT I DIDN'T PICK UP ANYTHING!
CHECK OUT
NO, BUT YOUR TREE DID.
YUM! WE THOUGHT IT MIGHT!
OW! I GET ALL THE GOOD JOBS!
BOUNCE
CRUMP!
OOM!
Then—
WHY HAVE YOU BROUGHT THAT ROTTEN TREE BACK, KIDS?
HE MADE US!
WELL, HE CAN JUST GET RID OF IT!
SIGH! WISH I HAD A SHARPER PENKNIFE.
SNIGGER! THAT'S THE LAST BOTANY LESSON WE'LL GET FOR A WEEK OR TWO.
SCRAPE!

TIME TO JOIN THE BASH STREET
WHAT'S
OLIVE'S DEMO.
MY POPCORN PIE MAKES A GREAT WEAPON.
POP! CRACK! POP!
SALT CELLAR

HOME ECONOMICS CLASS TO SEE...
COOKING?
SPLIT PEAS
DRIED ONION
DAMP LEEK
TEACHER ASKED US TO COOK A FEW RECIPES.
HEDGEHOG SUPREME.
COOK BOOK
ARGH! WHAT A FACE!
'ERBERT PICKED UP HIS MUM'S WASHING INSTEAD OF THE COOKING INGREDIENTS.
101 WAYS WITH EGGS
ALPHABET SOUP
SIMPLE AS ABC

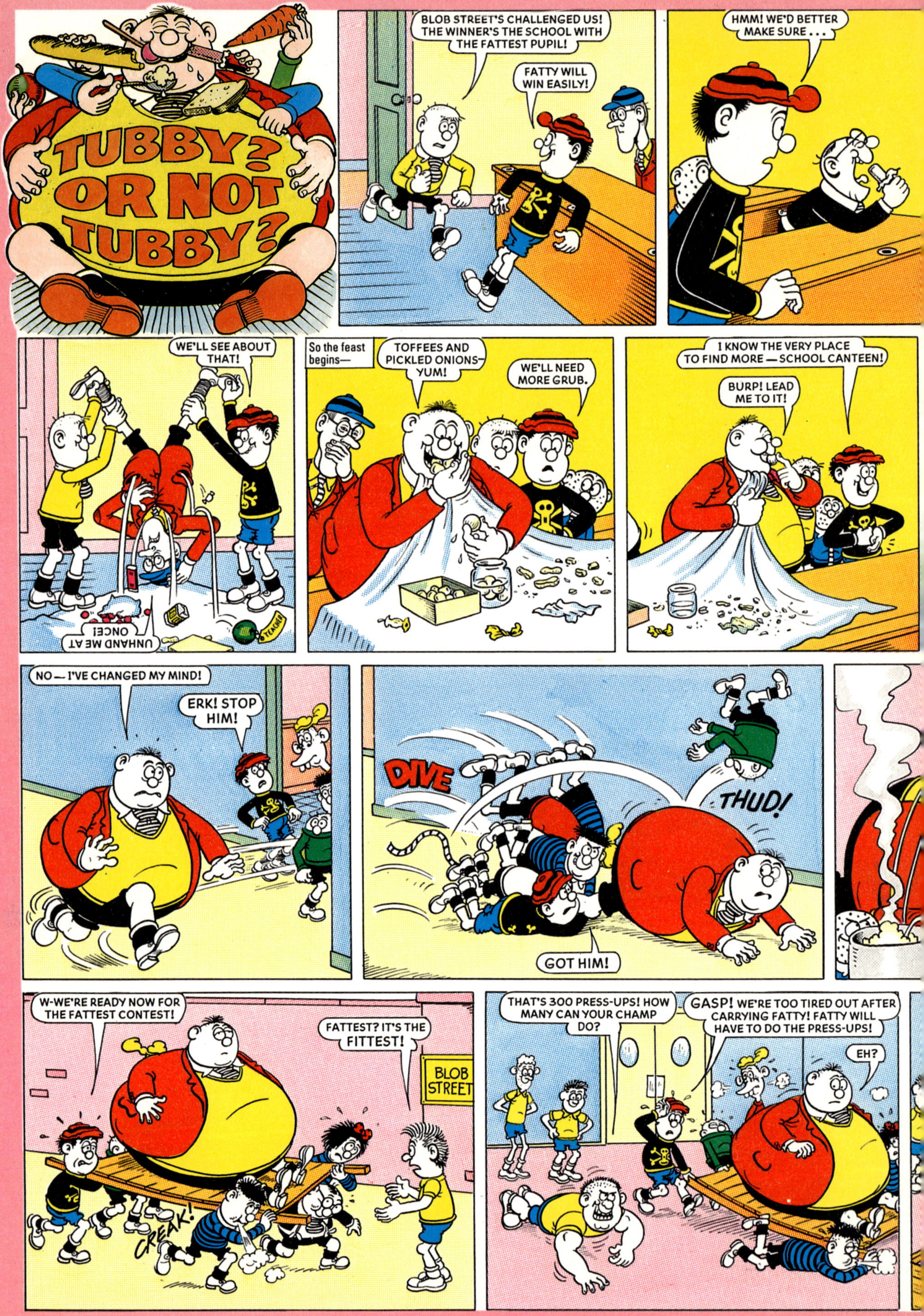
TUBBY? OR NOT TUBBY?
BLOB STREET'S CHALLENGED US! THE WINNER'S THE SCHOOL WITH THE FATTEST PUPIL!
FATTY WILL WIN EASILY!
HMM! WE'D BETTER MAKE SURE . . .
WE'LL SEE ABOUT THAT!
UNHAND ME AT ONCE!
So the feast begins—
TOFFEES AND PICKLED ONIONS— YUM!
WE'LL NEED MORE GRUB.
I KNOW THE VERY PLACE TO FIND MORE — SCHOOL CANTEEN!
BURP! LEAD ME TO IT!
NO — I'VE CHANGED MY MIND!
ERK! STOP HIM!
DIVE
THUD!
GOT HIM!
W-WE'RE READY NOW FOR THE FATTEST CONTEST!
FATTEST? IT'S THE FITTEST!
BLOB STREET
CREAK!
THAT'S 300 PRESS-UPS! HOW MANY CAN YOUR CHAMP DO?
GASP! WE'RE TOO TIRED OUT AFTER CARRYING FATTY! FATTY WILL HAVE TO DO THE PRESS-UPS!
EH?

. . . BY FEEDING FATTY ALL OF OUR GRUB!
MY SIGHT'S WORSE! I WAS SURE I HAD A CHOC BAR!
CLICK!
WE'VE GOT TO GET FATTY FATTER!
I'VE ONLY SUCKED THIS GOBSTOPPER ONCE!
HE CAN HAVE THIS — I'VE HAD IT IN MY POCKET FOR A MONTH.
WHAT ABOUT YOU, CUTHBERT?
THE FAT FOOL GETS NOTHING FROM ME!
LEAD YOU? NO — WE'LL CARRY YOU!
OTHERWISE YOU MIGHT EXERCISE OFF SOME OF THAT BEAUTEOUS FLAB!
NNNGH!
WHEW!
HOLD IT! YOU WANT ME TO EAT — THAT!
YES!
CURRY READY!
SUET FLAN READY!
MERCY!
CUSTARD READY!
TOO HORRIBLE TO BE SEEN BY ANYONE UNDER THE AGE OF 120!
NOW FOR THE CONTEST. FATTY'S IN GREAT SHAPE!
BOILK!
THAT'S IT FATTY — YOU CAN DO ONE!
NNNGGGH!
But—
HUH! ONE PRESS-UP! WHERE'S THAT OAF, SMIFFY?
I DON'T KNOW ABOUT FITTEST OR FATTEST BUT I CERTAINLY HOPE I'M THE FASTEST!
BASH STREET

GUESS WHAT! GUESS WHAT!
WHAT?
OO...ER...I FORGOT!
BLANK EXPRESSION
GROAN!
DIMWIT!
COME ON! OUT WITH IT!
S-H-A-K-E
WAIT! I REMEMBER!
TEST FOR PESTS
...NOBODY WOULD DREAM THAT MY DATES WERE IN HERE!
VIENNA ROLL
YUMMY! IT LOOKS NICE, DOESN'T IT?
SLURP
SLOO
At Wilfred's house —
I'VE GOT ALL MY DATES WRITTEN ON THE INSIDE OF MY JERSEY! EXCUSE ME POPPING INSIDE TO CHECK THEM!
SHRIEK! MY SON'S LOST HIS HEAD!
POP INSIDE
BED NO SUPPER, FOR SCARING THE WITS OUT OF YOUR DEAR OLD MUM — SHE DIDN'T HAVE MANY WITS TO START WITH!
HUMPH!
JABBER

WE'RE HAVING AN EXAM TOMORROW!
BET IT'S HISTORY!
VROOM
MUST GET HOME!
At 'Erbert's house —
GOOD PLAN TO WRITE ALL THE HISTORY DATES ON MY SPECS, EH!
HISTORY
MAKES IT A BIT HARD TO SEE VERY WELL, THOUGH! IN FACT, IT MAKES IT HARD TO SEE . . .
THUD
. . . AT ALL! OUCH!
SMASHING SUNSPECS, 'ERBERT!
I'M NOT WEARING ANY SPECS, MUM — THESE ARE BLACK EYES!
BUMP
'ERBERT'S MUM
At Fatty's house —
THESE ARE ALL THE POSSIBLE ANSWERS FOR THE EXAM AND I'VE GOT THE PERFECT HIDING PLACE . . .
1 DOZ PIES
1 DOZ PIES
1 DOZ PIES
WATERLOO 1815 HADRIAN'S WALL BUILT 121 A.D. JULIUS CEASAR LANDED 55 BC AGINCOURT 1415 STEVENSONS ROCKET 1829 BATTLE OF HASTINGS 1066
One munching later —
GROAN! I'M NEVER EVER GOING TO EAT 500 DATES AT ONE SITTING AGAIN!
At Plug's house —
I'M GOING TO WRITE MY DATES ON MY TEETH . . .
. . . IF I CAN GET A MIRROR TO STAY WHOLE LONG ENOUGH TO WRITE THEM!
SHATTER
Next day —
HURRY UP, CHILDREN — IT'S YOUR EXAMINATION TODAY!
WE KNOW!
THE DOCTOR WILL BE WAITING!
GROAN! A MEDICAL EXAM? WE SHOULD HAVE OUR HEADS EXAMINED FOR LISTENING TO DAFT SMIFFY!
WE WANT A DATE WITH YOU, SMIFFY!
ULP! I'LL NEED A MEDICAL EXAM IF THAT LOT CATCH UP WITH ME!
ZOOM

The Leader of the Pack

THE BASH STREET PUPS

PIE FEVER

A poem by the ~~lard~~... er BARD of Bash Street.

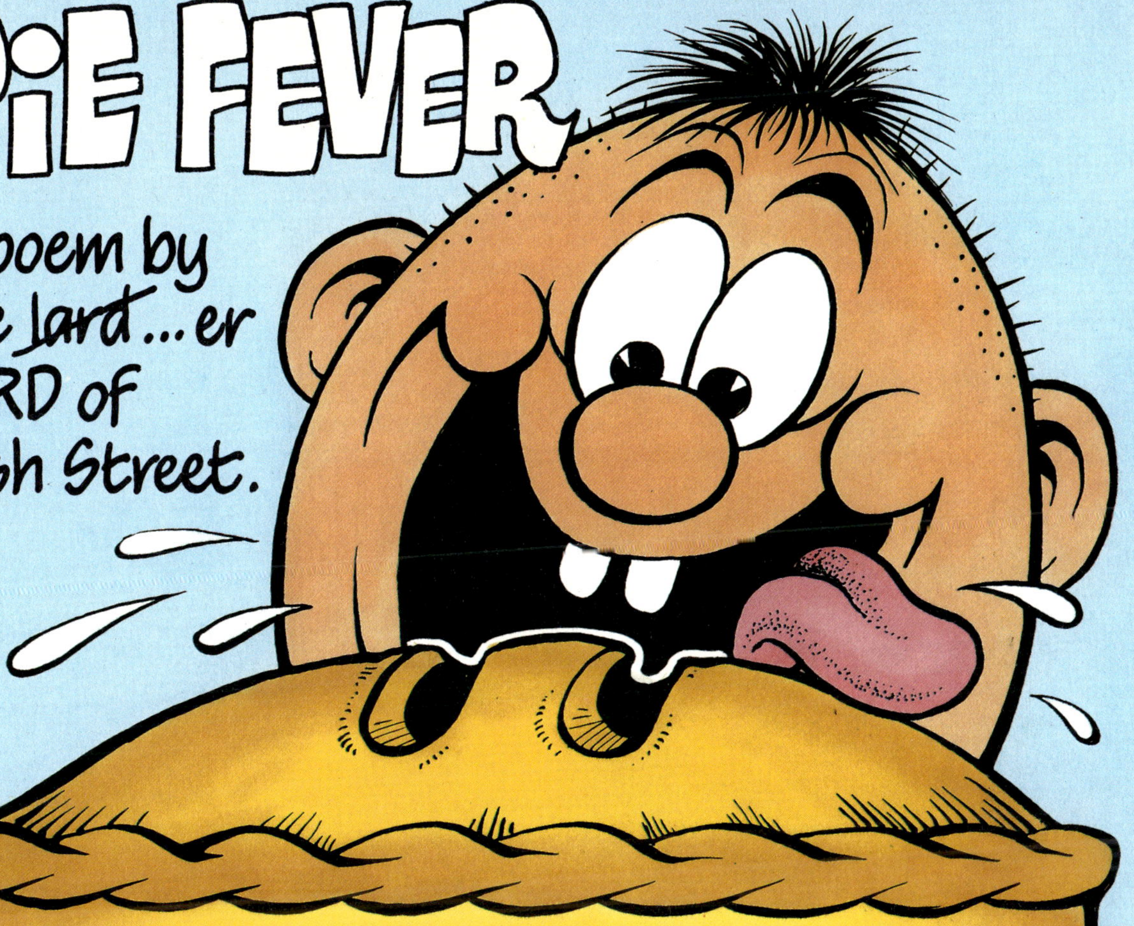

I must go home for my tea again, for the lovely sight of a pie,
For I'm a pie fanatic and here I'll tell you why;
A mince pie, a bean pie, a pie all filled with curry,
Whatever size or shape it is, I'll eat it in a hurry.

I must go home for my tea again, for the call of my rumbling tum
Is a loud call and a rude call, that upsets everyone;
And what I need is a huge feed to pass across my lips,
Like a steak pie with brown sauce and a massive pile of chips.

I've just got home for my tea again, to a frightening surprise,
My daft mum's made a salad, instead of the usual pies;
When I refuse to eat it, Mum calls me a disgrace,
So I eat the salad all in one — placed in a large pie case!

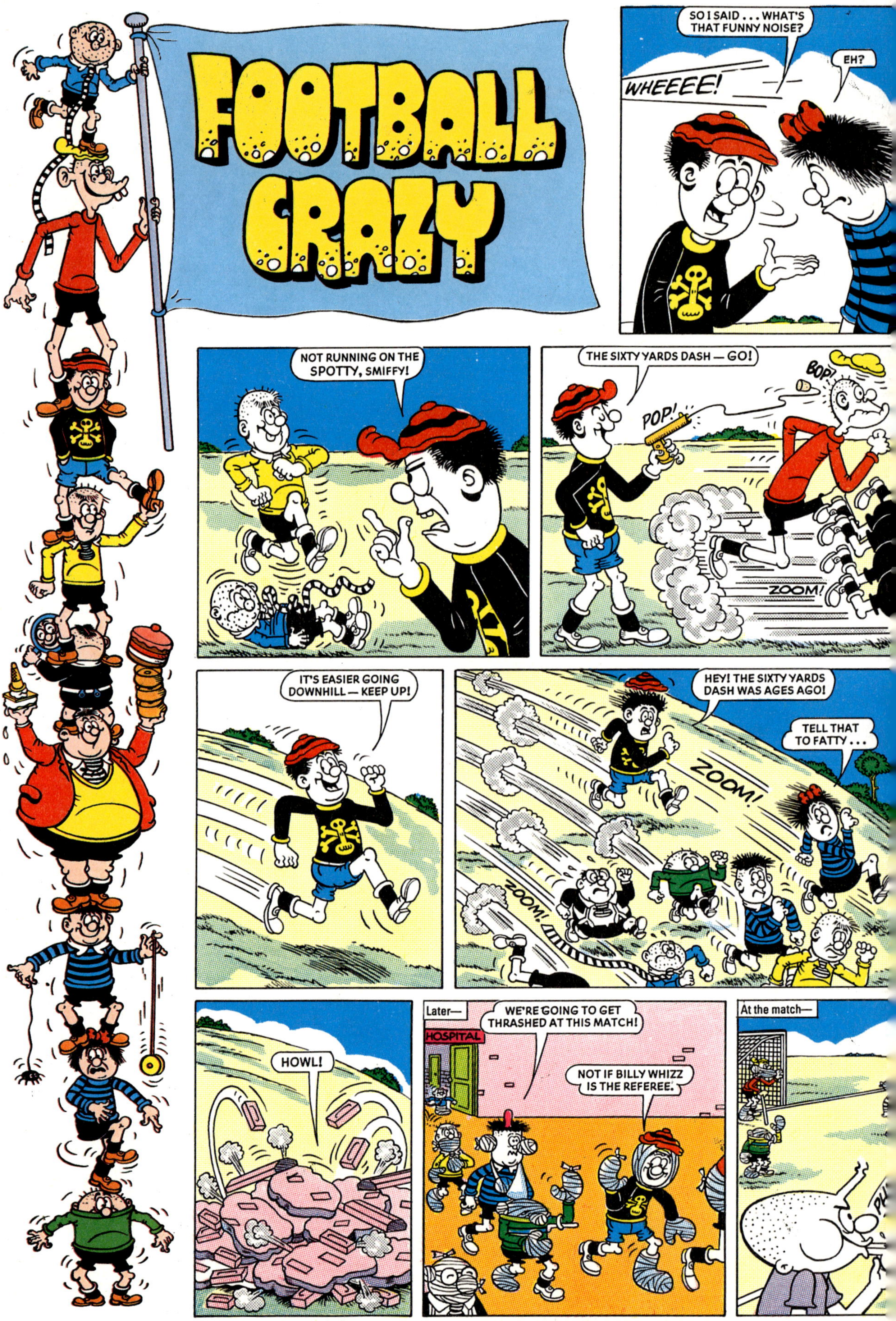
FOOTBALL CRAZY
SO I SAID . . . WHAT'S THAT FUNNY NOISE?
WHEEEEE!
EH?
NOT RUNNING ON THE SPOTTY, SMIFFY!
THE SIXTY YARDS DASH — GO!
POP!
BOP!
ZOOM!
IT'S EASIER GOING DOWNHILL — KEEP UP!
HEY! THE SIXTY YARDS DASH WAS AGES AGO!
TELL THAT TO FATTY . . .
ZOOM!
ZOOM!
HOWL!
Later—
HOSPITAL
WE'RE GOING TO GET THRASHED AT THIS MATCH!
NOT IF BILLY WHIZZ IS THE REFEREE.
At the match—

LOOK! THERE'S WRITING ON IT . . .
OW!
. . . SEE?
WE CHALLENGE YOU TO A FOOTBALL MATCH Signed Blob St.
WE'LL HAVE TO GO INTO TRAINING TO GET FIT. RUNNING ON THE SPOT BEGIN!
GASP!
WHEEZE!
WE'D BETTER MAKE THAT THE FIVE YARDS DASH, TEN YARDS STAGGER AND FORTY FIVE YARDS CRAWL!
GROAN!
Later—
A CROSS-COUNTRY RUN WILL GET US FIT! LET'S GO!
WHIMPER!
TUMBLE
OOER!
. . . HE TRIPPED!
ABANDON CROSS-COUNTRY RUN! WOMEN AND ME FIRST!
STAMP
STAMP
T-TRAPPED!
SICKENING
BONE-CRUNCHING
SQUELCH!
CRACK!
CRACK!
THIS'LL BE TOO EASY!
F-FULL TIME? B-BUT WE'VE JUST G-GOT ST-STARTED!
PHEEP!
THAT'S WHY WE NEEDED BILLY TO REFEREE — HIS WATCH GOES AS FAST AS HE DOES!
B-ZZZZZZZ

WELL, WELL, WELL!
TEACHER RUSHING TO GET TO SCHOOL? MOST UNUSUAL.
HE MUST BE ILL!
Next —
NOW WHY DID HE DO THAT?
TINKLE! CLINK!
THANK YOU, HEADMASTER.
CLASS IIB
CHORTLE!
SWEEP UP
Then —
HERE'S A LETTER FOR TEACHER. IT'S ALL THE WAY FROM AMERICA.
CLASS IIB
LISTEN TO THIS, TEACHER! YOU'VE BEEN LEFT TWO OIL WELLS BY YOUR GREAT UNCLE HANK IN TEXAS!
COO!
EH?
DAZZLE
ER . . . WHERE DID YOU GET ALL THE CASH TO PAY FOR THIS, DEAR? DID YOU GET A WAGE INCREASE?
NO! I'LL PAY LATER! I'LL USE A TINY BIT OF THE CASH MY OIL WELLS ARE GOING TO EARN FOR ME!
I DON'T THINK YOU'LL GET THAT MUCH IF YOU SELL THESE OIL WELL ORNAMENTS! THEY ARRIVED FROM TEXAS THIS MORNING!
HEH-HEH!

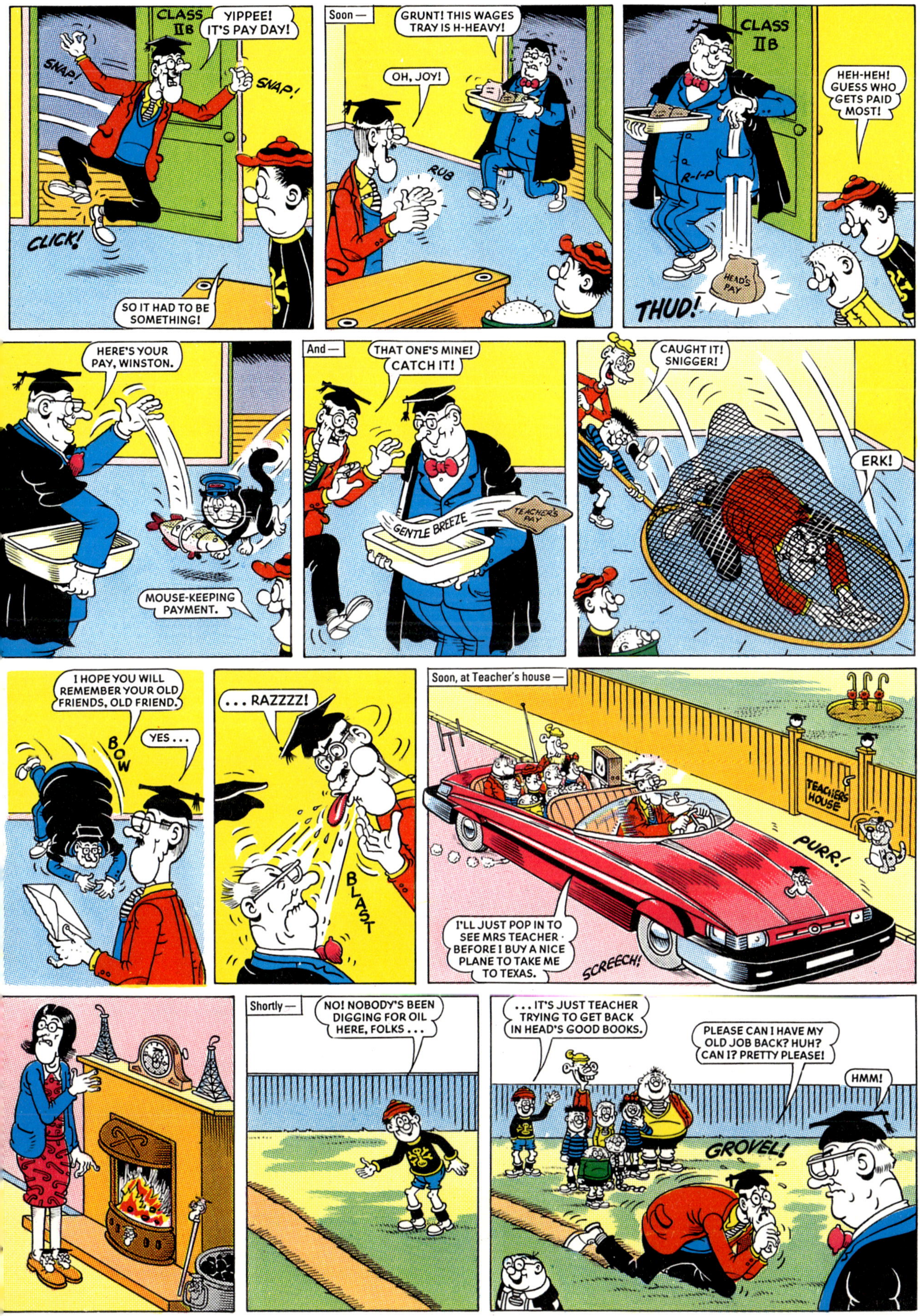
CLASS IIB
YIPPEE! IT'S PAY DAY!
SNAP!
SNAP!
CLICK!
SO IT HAD TO BE SOMETHING!
Soon —
GRUNT! THIS WAGES TRAY IS H-HEAVY!
OH, JOY!
RUB
CLASS IIB
HEH-HEH! GUESS WHO GETS PAID MOST!
R-I-P
HEAD'S PAY
THUD!
HERE'S YOUR PAY, WINSTON.
MOUSE-KEEPING PAYMENT.
And —
THAT ONE'S MINE! CATCH IT!
GENTLE BREEZE
TEACHER'S PAY
CAUGHT IT! SNIGGER!
ERK!
I HOPE YOU WILL REMEMBER YOUR OLD FRIENDS, OLD FRIEND.
BOW
YES . . .
. . . RAZZZZ!
BLAST
Soon, at Teacher's house —
TEACHER'S HOUSE
PURR!
I'LL JUST POP IN TO SEE MRS TEACHER BEFORE I BUY A NICE PLANE TO TAKE ME TO TEXAS.
SCREECH!
Shortly —
NO! NOBODY'S BEEN DIGGING FOR OIL HERE, FOLKS . . .
. . . IT'S JUST TEACHER TRYING TO GET BACK IN HEAD'S GOOD BOOKS.
PLEASE CAN I HAVE MY OLD JOB BACK? HUH? CAN I? PRETTY PLEASE!
HMM!
GROVEL!

WE'LL MEET AGAIN
HEY! I HEARD TEACHER'S GOING TO GIVE EXTRA HOMEWORK.
WE'LL HAVE A SECRET MEETING TO DECIDE WHAT TO DO.
UP HERE SHOULD BE SECRET ENOUGH!
So—
FOLLOW ME.
THIS SHOULD BE SAFE FROM PRYING EARS.
STOP BREATHING DOWN MY NECK, PLUG.
IT'S NOT ME! I'M OVER HERE!
WH-WHAT'S HAPPENING?
WE'RE MOVING!
Here's why—
HEAVY BIN, THIS!
IN IT GOES.
NOBODY WILL COME CLOSE ENOUGH TO LISTEN TO OUR SECRET MEETING NOW.
WHAT A NIFF!
GASP!
FOR SALE
Later—
WE HEAR YOU'RE GOING TO GIVE EXTRA HOMEWORK.
THAT'S RIGHT!

So—
I CALL THIS MEETING TO ORDER!
CAN I ORDER CHIPS?
W-WE'RE SINKING.
HMPH! THIS MEETING ISN'T VERY SECRET!
IT'S YOUR FAULT, FATTY—YOUR WEIGHT'S SUNK THE LAMP POST!
CHEEK!
THEN WHO . . ? OOOOO!
SNORT!
I'M SURE THERE WERE SOME KIDS HERE A SECOND AGO!
ZIP!
VROOOM!
Later—
JUST THE MEETING PLACE WE'RE LOOKING FOR.
LET US OUT!
RUBBISH TIP
COMPOST COMPANY
B-BUT NOT HERE!
CABBAGE GRADE 13
KIPPERS SELL BY MAY '87
I'M GIVING IT TO MY FAVOURITE, BEST, PRIZE PUPIL, CUTHBERT!
NOT TO US?
PONG!
DON'T BE DAFT! I COULDN'T STAND SEEING ANY MORE OF YOUR HOMEWORK!
Soon—
ULP! NOW THE K-KIDS W-WANT A SECRET MEETING W-WITH ME!

What shall we do with THE SLEEPING TEACHER
Sung to the tune of "THE DRUNKEN SAILOR"
What shall we do with a sleeping teacher?
What shall we do with a sleeping teacher?
What shall we do with a sleeping teacher?
Ear-ly in the morning!
Chorus
Wa-hey! We've got surprises!
Wa-hey! We've got surprises!
Wa-hey! We've got surprises!
Ear-ly in the morning!
DAB!
Paint him on the face with Toots' lipstick!
Paint him on the face with Toots' lipstick!
Paint him on the face with Toots' lipstick!
Ear-ly in the morning!
(Repeat chorus).
Hoo-ray! We're going home early!
Hoo-ray! We're going home early!
Hoo-ray! We're going home early!
Ear-ly in the morning!

Feed the birds with his tea-time biscuits!
Feed the birds with his tea-time biscuits!
Feed the birds with his tea-time biscuits!
Ear-ly in the morning!
(Repeat chorus).
PIZZA DELIVERY
Spend all his money on take-away pizzas!
Spend all his money on take-away pizzas!
Spend all his money on take-away pizzas!
Ear-ly in the morning!
(Repeat chorus).
POUR
BANG!
Fill his shoes with Olive's custard!
Fill his shoes with Olive's custard!
Fill his shoes with Olive's custard!
Ear-ly in the morning!
(Repeat chorus).
THUMP
Tie him to his desk by his moustache hairs!
Tie him to his desk by his moustache hairs!
Tie him to his desk by his moustache hairs!
Ear-ly in the morning!
(Repeat chorus).

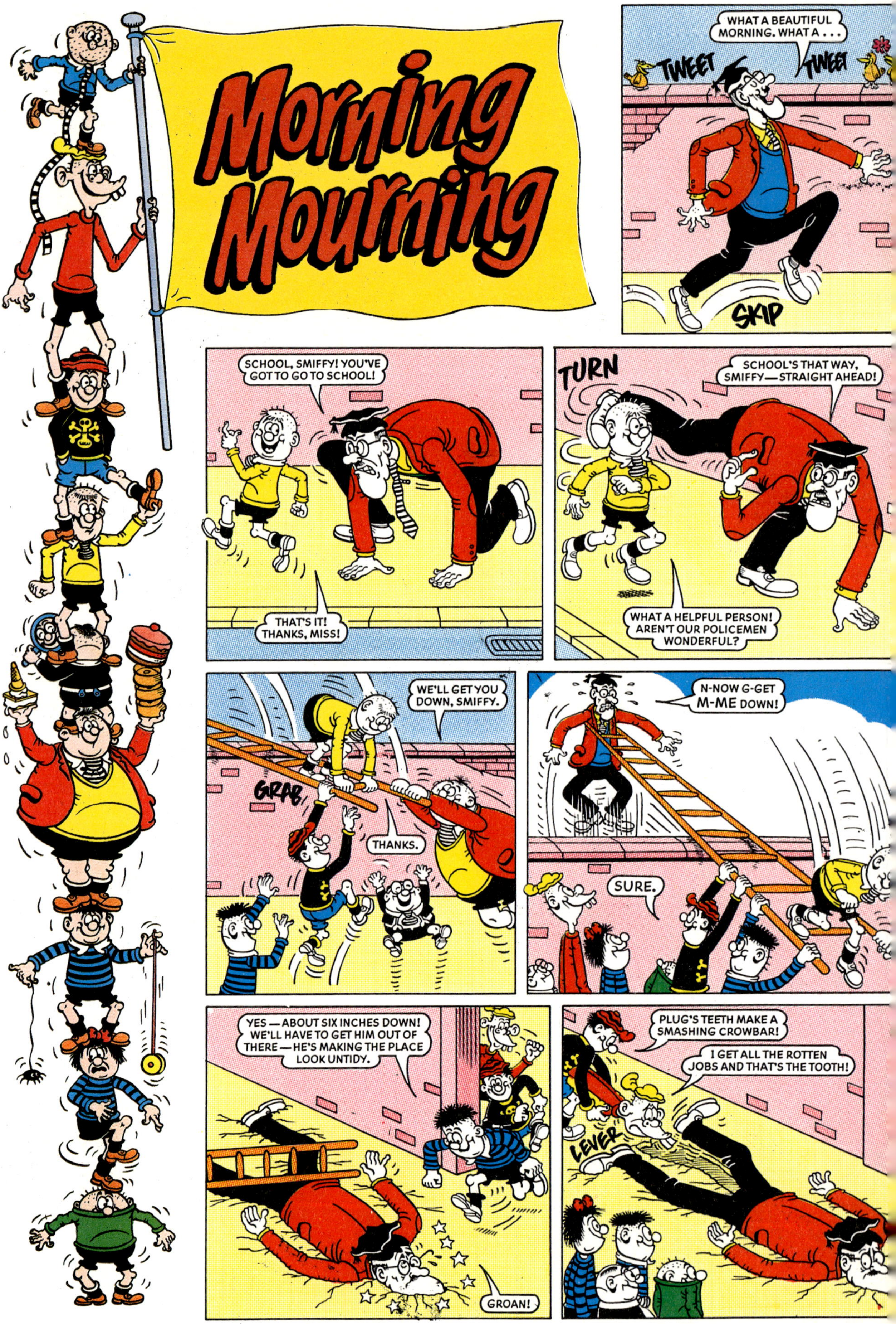
Morning Mourning
WHAT A BEAUTIFUL MORNING. WHAT A . . .
TWEET
TWEET
SKIP
SCHOOL, SMIFFY! YOU'VE GOT TO GO TO SCHOOL!
THAT'S IT! THANKS, MISS!
TURN
SCHOOL'S THAT WAY, SMIFFY—STRAIGHT AHEAD!
WHAT A HELPFUL PERSON! AREN'T OUR POLICEMEN WONDERFUL?
WE'LL GET YOU DOWN, SMIFFY.
GRAB
THANKS.
N-NOW G-GET M-ME DOWN!
SURE.
YES—ABOUT SIX INCHES DOWN! WE'LL HAVE TO GET HIM OUT OF THERE—HE'S MAKING THE PLACE LOOK UNTIDY.
GROAN!
PLUG'S TEETH MAKE A SMASHING CROWBAR!
I GET ALL THE ROTTEN JOBS AND THAT'S THE TOOTH!
LEVER

WALLOP!
. . . P-PAIN IN THE CHIN! OOYAH!
WHY ARE YOU SITTING IN THE MIDDLE OF THE PAVEMENT? HMM?
I'M SURE I'VE GOT SOMETHING TO DO, BUT I CAN'T THINK WHAT — SO SHHHH!
TEACHER DID SAY STRAIGHT AHEAD!
ERK!
SILLY PUPIL! YOU'RE GOING TO HURT SOMEBODY!
N-NAMELY ME!
BASH STREET SCHOOL
ARGH!
WHUMP
HE'S DOWN!
TREMBLE
SHAKE
THERE! YOU'RE NOT DOWN AND IN ANYMORE, TEACHER — YOU'RE UP AND OUT!
LIFT
MOAN!
Then —
WHAT A BEAUTIFUL MORNING — WHAT . . .
THE HEAD
BASH ST SCHOOL
. . . DID I SAY? WHAT DID I DO?
BAH!

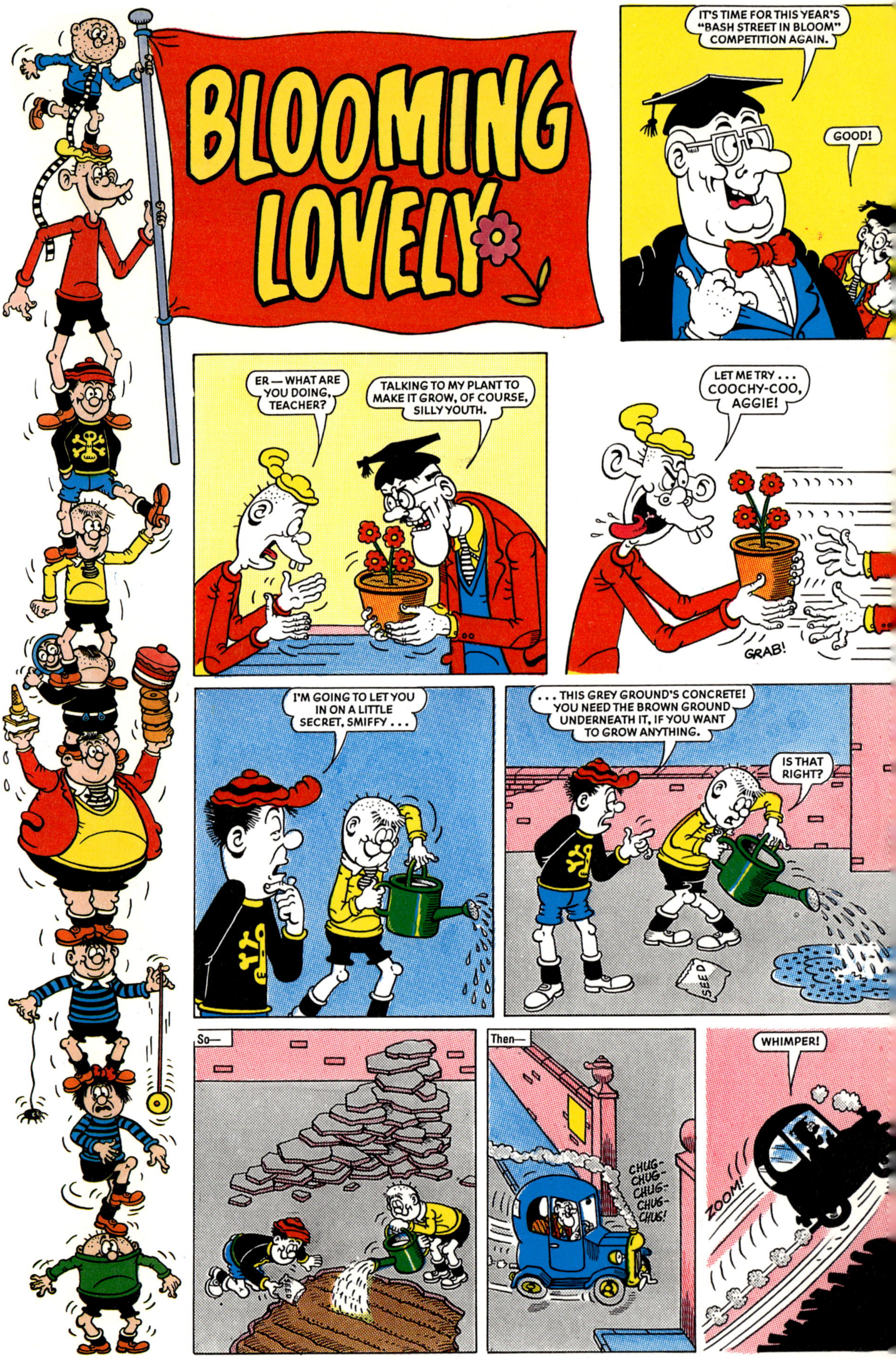
BLOOMING LOVELY
IT'S TIME FOR THIS YEAR'S "BASH STREET IN BLOOM" COMPETITION AGAIN.
GOOD!
ER — WHAT ARE YOU DOING, TEACHER?
TALKING TO MY PLANT TO MAKE IT GROW, OF COURSE, SILLY YOUTH.
LET ME TRY . . . COOCHY-COO, AGGIE!
GRAB!
I'M GOING TO LET YOU IN ON A LITTLE SECRET, SMIFFY . . .
. . . THIS GREY GROUND'S CONCRETE! YOU NEED THE BROWN GROUND UNDERNEATH IT, IF YOU WANT TO GROW ANYTHING.
IS THAT RIGHT?
SEED
So—
SEED
Then—
CHUG-CHUG-CHUG-CHUG-CHUG!
WHIMPER!
ZOOM!

BECAUSE I'M GOING TO WIN IT THIS YEAR . . .
SAFE
. . . WITH THE HELP OF AGATHA.
SAFE
BEAUTIFUL AGATHA, LOVE OF MY LIFE, PASSION OF MY . . .
TEACHER'S GONE FLOWER-POTTY!
BLEH!
AGH! YOUR FACE HAS DONE FOR AGATHA, YOU ROTTER!
WILT!
BOO-HOO!
WE'LL WIN "BASH STREET IN BLOOM" AND MAKE TEACHER HAPPY AGAIN.
Next morning—
I'M SCATTERING THE FLOWER SEEDS.
I LIKE MY FLOUR AND SEEDS IN A SEED CAKE!
SEED
HOW DO I GET TO THE BROWN GROUND?
I CAN'T THINK OF EVERYTHING — USE YOUR HEAD FOR ONCE!
OK!
THUD!
EEK! I DIDN'T MEAN . . .
. . . STILL, IT WORKED! NOW WE CAN PLANT OUR SEEDS!
DAZED
LOOK WHERE TEACHER'S LANDED! FETCH EARTH, SEEDS AND WATER! I'VE GOT A GREAT IDEA!
Later—
BEST HANGING FLOWER BASKET I'VE EVER SEEN.
WELL, WE WON THE COMPETITION FOR TEACHER, BUT SOMETIMES THERE'S JUST NO PLEASING HIM!
RANT! RAVE!

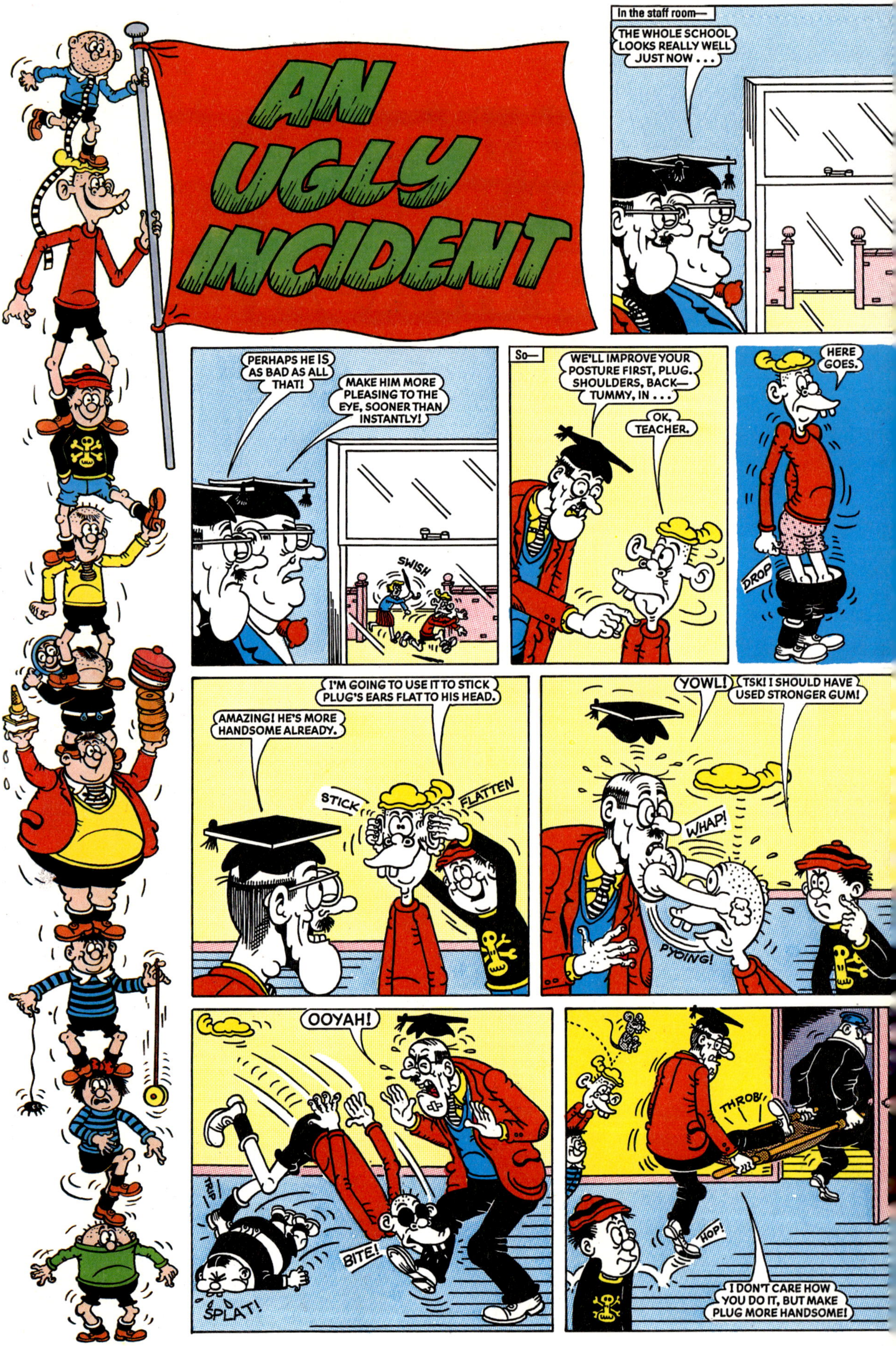
AN UGLY INCIDENT
In the staff room—
THE WHOLE SCHOOL LOOKS REALLY WELL JUST NOW . . .
PERHAPS HE IS AS BAD AS ALL THAT!
MAKE HIM MORE PLEASING TO THE EYE, SOONER THAN INSTANTLY!
SWISH
So—
WE'LL IMPROVE YOUR POSTURE FIRST, PLUG. SHOULDERS, BACK— TUMMY, IN . . .
OK, TEACHER.
HERE GOES.
DROP
I'M GOING TO USE IT TO STICK PLUG'S EARS FLAT TO HIS HEAD.
AMAZING! HE'S MORE HANDSOME ALREADY.
STICK
FLATTEN
YOWL!
TSK! I SHOULD HAVE USED STRONGER GUM!
WHAP!
P'YOING!
OOYAH!
TRIP
BITE!
SPLAT!
THROB!
HOP!
I DON'T CARE HOW YOU DO IT, BUT MAKE PLUG MORE HANDSOME!

. . . EXCEPT F-FOR THAT UNLOVELY Y-YOUTH!
COME NOW, HEAD! HE'S NOT AS BAD AS ALL THAT!
Meanwhile—
NOW, FIDO — LET'S HAVE A NICE PEACEFUL WALKY.
WHAT A NICE FAMILY.
THUD!
WAH!
HOWL!
GOOD MORNING!
AHEM! WE'LL — ER — SKIP THE POSTURE JUST NOW.
BLUSH
SNIGGER!
CEASE THIS UNSEEMLY MIRTH — YOU CAN HELP MAKE PLUG BEAUTIFUL!
Y-YOU MUST BE JOKING! CACKLE!
OK, I'LL HELP, BUT I'VE GOT TO CHEW THIS FIRST.
HOW CAN CHEWING GUM HELP?
I'VE GOT A BETTER IDEA.
HOI!
POP STARS WEAR "SHADES" TO MAKE THEMSELVES LOOK MUCH MORE HANDSOME!
THAT'S ALL VERY WELL, BUT . . .
SPLOT!
. . . I CAN'T SEE A THING!
NEITHER CAN I!
THIS IS WORSE THAN VERY, VERY HARD SUMS!
In the staff room—
TEACHER, WE'VE DONE IT . . .
GOOD!
TEACHER'S PET
. . . BUT I DON'T THINK PLUG'S TOO HAPPY ABOUT IT!
CHEEK!
SIGH! I SUPPOSE IT'S THE BEST YOU COULD DO.

CARPET CAPERS

WITH THE BASH STREET PUPS

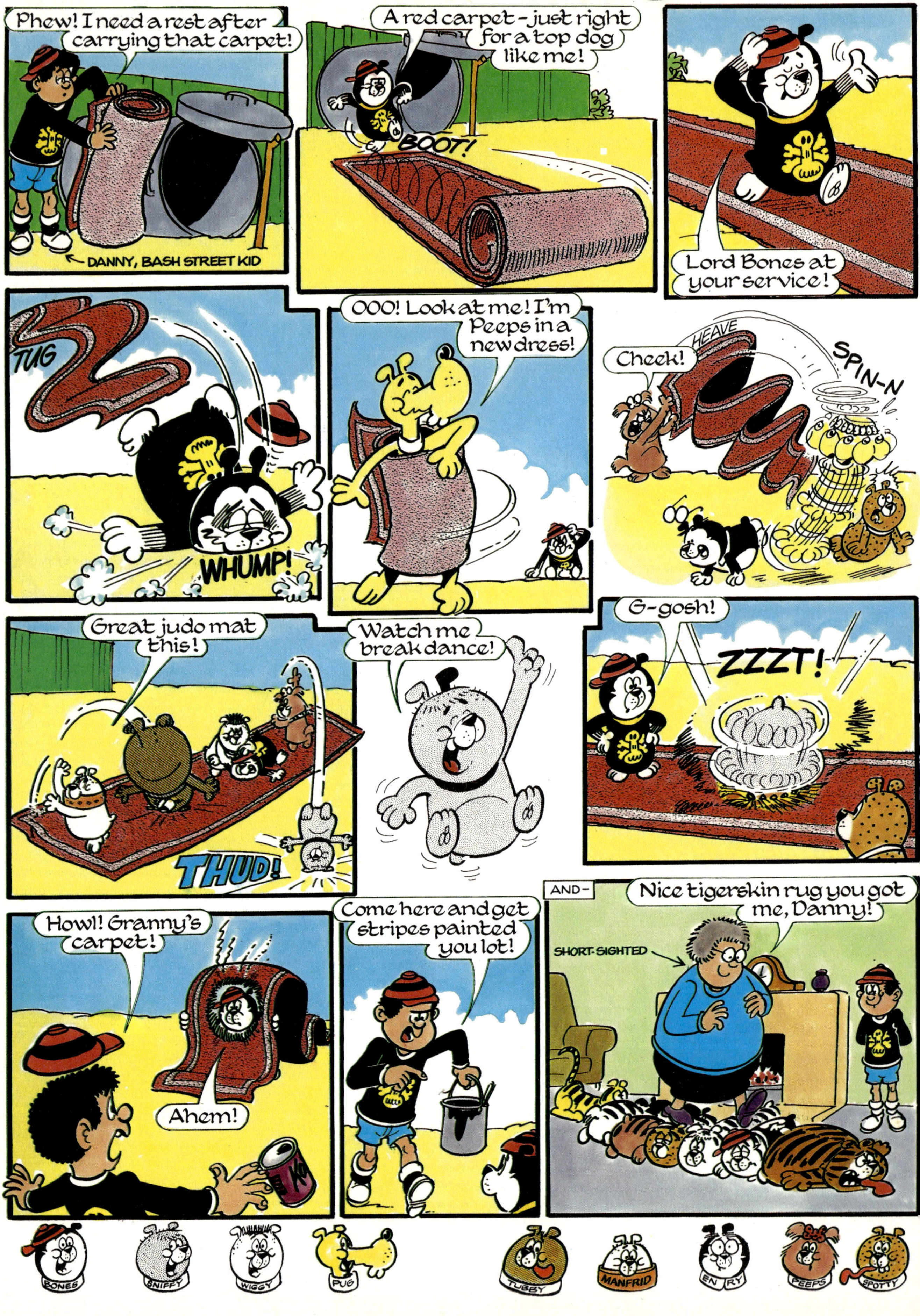

TRY OUR MOUSE ~~CROSS~~WORD!

CLUES:-

Across

2. Disney's famous mouse! (6)
3. The only thing we mice have in common with cats. We both have -------- on our faces! (8)
5. Three ----- ----. Complete the famous nursery rhyme title. (5-4)
7. A type of 6 DOWN. (7)
10. The animal we mice hate most! (3)
11. The noise mice make. (6)

Down

1. Tom's partner. (5)
3. The Bash St. cat who can't catch us! (7)
4. What the mouse in 8 DOWN ran up. (5)
6. Our favourite food. (6)
8. Hickory, Dickory, ----? (4)
9. Our big cousins. (4)

Answers

Across:- Mickey; Whiskers; Blind Mice; Cheddar; Cat; Squeak.
Down:- Jerry; Winston; Clock; Cheese; Dock; Rats.

OFF THE WALL FUN
THE ETON WALL GAME HAS BEEN A TRADITION AT ETON COLLEGE FOR HUNDREDS OF YEARS.
ONLY ABOUT ONE GOAL A CENTURY IS SCORED!
COO! IMAGINE THAT . . .
I KNOW—LET'S INVENT A BASH STREET WALL GAME!
RIGHT—I'LL TRY AND HIT THE STUMPS WITH THIS FOOTBALL! YOU ATTEMPT TO HIT IT INTO THE NETBALL NET FOR A GOAL!
OK!
So—
HERE IT COMES!
Then—
WHAP!
CHEEK?
KICK!
GASP!
In the boiler room—
NO EXCEPTIONS, FATTY! THE MELTED TOFFEE BARS WILL MAKE GREAT CEMENT!
HEAT
And—
HOI! FATTY! STOP SUCKING THAT BRICK AND BRING IT OVER HERE!
SUCK!
THERE—IT SHOULD BE DRY WHEN WE COME OUT AGAIN.

ZZZ! EH? WHAT?
A GOAL!
YAWN! A GOAL? WHAT'S A GOAL?
At interval—
SCHOOL
WHAT WILL WE PLAY TODAY?
CRICKET!
FOOTBALL!
TENNIS!
NETBALL!
Will it be a goal?
No!
GLUMPH!
Next—
ERK! MY CANDYFLOSS!
HUH! IT'LL BE ABOUT A HUNDRED YEARS TILL ANYONE SCORES IN THE BASH STREET WALL GAME!
ERK!
SPLAT!
WE'LL HAVE TO REBUILD THE WALL!
BUT WE'VE NO CEMENT!
RIGHT—EVERYONE GIVE ME THEIR TOFFEE BARS!
JUST IN TIME—THERE'S THE SCHOOL BELL.
And later—
SCHOOL
RIGHT—NOW FOR ANOTHER GAME!
TUG
CHEW!
CHOMP! SLURP!
BAH! LOOKS LIKE IT'S THE EATEN WALL GAME NOW!

That's Showbiz!
THIS IS BORING! BORING!
SCHOOLS' PROGRAMME
21
39
148
WONDER WHAT ELSE IS ON?
HOI!
PLINK! PLUNK! PLONK!
I HAVE MUSICAL TEETH!
But—
ENOUGH! ENOUGH!
YAROO!
JAB
I'M A VENTRILOQUIST! BET YOU CAN'T SEE MY LIPS MOVE!
RIGHT, SMIFFY—WRITE DOWN A NUMBER!
WHISPER:—SMIFFY CAN'T COUNT PAST ONE, SO THAT MUST BE THE NUMBER!
THE NUMBER IS ONE!
NO, YOU'RE WRONG!
IT'S RED!
RED
IDIOT—THAT'S A COLOUR, NOT A NUMBER!
IS THERE ANYONE WHO CAN IMPROVE ON THIS?
ERK!
SNAP!
SNAP!
TAP DANCING? TRAP DANCING'S MORE LIKE IT!
AAIIEEE!
THROB
THROB
Plug tries singing—
WAIL! SCREECH!

MA! SHE'S BAKING PIES FOR ME....
COO! IT'S LENA MACARONI, THE CHILD STAR!
SHE'S GREAT!
WISH WE COULD GET INTO SHOW BUSINESS!
STARS IN THEIR EYES
PLUG AND I HAVE FORMED A MUSICAL DUO!
REALLY?
BREAD AND BUTTER! BREAD AND BUTTER!
GASP! DANNY'S BRILLIANT!
But—
TRRINNG!
INTERVAL! YAHOO!
BAH! IT'S 'ERBERT IN DISGUISE!
Soon—
SMIFFY AND I WILL DO A MIND-READING ACT!
I CAN TAP DANCE!
TAP! TAP! TAP!
TIME I DID SOMETHING ABOUT THOSE NOISY MICE!
THESE WILL GET RID OF THEM!
WHAT'S WRONG, SONNY? YOU SOUND IN DREADFUL PAIN!
WAIL! HOWL!
PROD
But—
SCHOOL
SIGN HERE, SON—YOUR VOICE WILL MAKE YOUR FORTUNE!
CONTRACT
HOWL! MOAN!
GASP! HE MUST BE A SHOW BUSINESS AGENT! PLUG'S GOING TO BE A CHILD STAR!
But—
LATE FINAL! GET YOUR PAPER HERE!
"BEANO" TOWN NEWS
LATE NIGHT FINAL
HAW-HAW-HAW!

TEACHER'S PET HATES!
WHEN 'ERBERT CLEANS HIS GLASSES!
BRIGHT SUNSHINE
4
+5
WHEN TOOTS WEARS HER PERSONAL STEREO!
YOWL!
SHRIEK! MY CAR!
GASP! WHAT AN UGLY FACE!
BIN CART
CRUNCH!
WHEN PLUG LOOKS OUT THE WINDOW!

WHEN SID BRINGS ONE OF HIS PETS TO SCHOOL!
TEACHER'S A TWIT! TEACHER'S A TWIT!
PARROT SEEDS
WHEN FATTY EATS IN CLASS!
GUZZLE!
CRISPS
WHEN CUTHBERT INTERRUPTS!
SURELY YOU KNOW THE SQUARE OF THE HYPOTENUSE IS EQUAL TO THE SUM OF THE SQUARES OF THE OTHER TWO SIDES . . .
25
16
9
LOOKS LIKE TEACHER'S PET HATE IS TEACHER'S PET!

"OUT" FOR FUN!
ARE YOU GOING TO BE A PAINTER AND DECORATOR, TEACHER?
CLASS IIB
GRR! NO! I'M TRYING TO GET INTO THE TEACHER'S CRICKET TEAM!
NOW YOU'RE THE SILLY MID — OFF!
OOYAH!
GENTLE TWHACK
THERE'S A JOLLY OLD RUN THERE, I THINK!
THUMP!
WHAT DO YOU CALL IT WHEN SOMEONE'S OUT FOR NO RUNS?
But—
WHO NEEDS HANDS?
AN AARDVARK?
FLIP
FLIP
OUT!
I AM NOT! HE DIDN'T CATCH IT WITH HIS HAND! ANYWAY . . .
. . . THIS IS MY BAT AND BALL!
GRR! WHY DID YOU TELL ME TO DUCK?
CLICK!
I DIDN'T! THAT'S WHAT YOU'RE OUT FOR!
I HOPE YOU'LL STILL CONSIDER ME, NICE TEACHERS!
GROVEL
DON'T WORRY — THERE'S A POSITION FOR YOU!

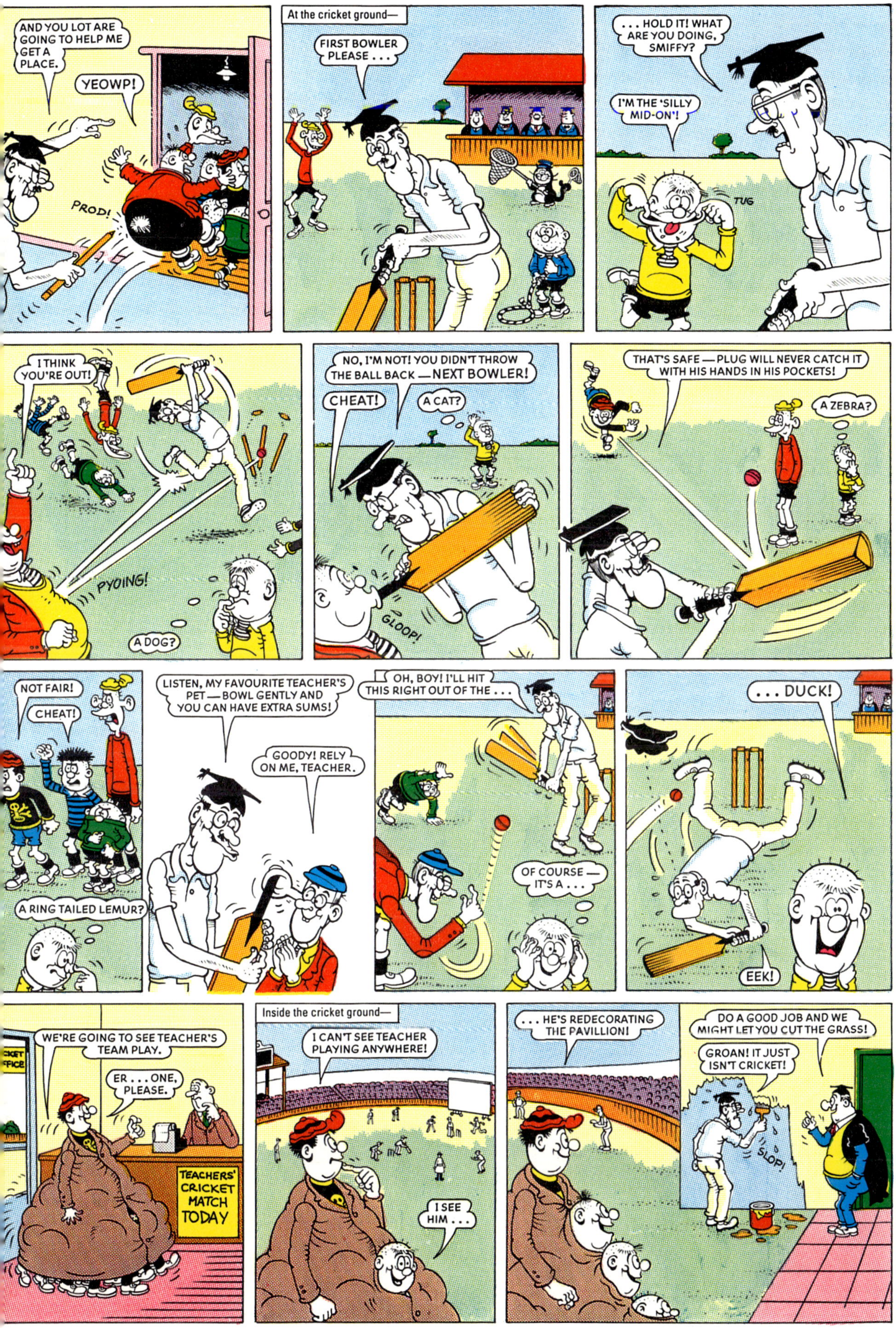
AND YOU LOT ARE GOING TO HELP ME GET A PLACE.
YEOWP!
PROD!
At the cricket ground—
FIRST BOWLER PLEASE . . .
. . . HOLD IT! WHAT ARE YOU DOING, SMIFFY?
I'M THE 'SILLY MID-ON'!
TUG
I THINK YOU'RE OUT!
PYOING!
A DOG?
NO, I'M NOT! YOU DIDN'T THROW THE BALL BACK — NEXT BOWLER!
CHEAT!
A CAT?
GLOOP!
THAT'S SAFE — PLUG WILL NEVER CATCH IT WITH HIS HANDS IN HIS POCKETS!
A ZEBRA?
NOT FAIR!
CHEAT!
A RING TAILED LEMUR?
LISTEN, MY FAVOURITE TEACHER'S PET — BOWL GENTLY AND YOU CAN HAVE EXTRA SUMS!
GOODY! RELY ON ME, TEACHER.
OH, BOY! I'LL HIT THIS RIGHT OUT OF THE . . .
OF COURSE — IT'S A . . .
. . . DUCK!
EEK!
WE'RE GOING TO SEE TEACHER'S TEAM PLAY.
ER . . . ONE, PLEASE.
TEACHERS' CRICKET MATCH TODAY
Inside the cricket ground—
I CAN'T SEE TEACHER PLAYING ANYWHERE!
I SEE HIM . . .
. . . HE'S REDECORATING THE PAVILLION!
DO A GOOD JOB AND WE MIGHT LET YOU CUT THE GRASS!
GROAN! IT JUST ISN'T CRICKET!
SLOP!

BOXING CLEVER
I SAY I'M THE MOST PEACEFUL PUPIL!
NONSENSE! I AM!
DON'T TALK RUBBISH! I AM!
I'M THE MOST PEACEFUL! OUCH!
TAKE THAT!
IT'S ME!
I AM!
I KNOW HOW TO WIN—PUT HORSESHOES IN YOUR BOXING GLOVES!
SCHOOL DUNCE— ALWAYS GETS THINGS WRONG
SMART THINKING FOR ONCE, SMIFFY!
Presently—
LOUD WHINNY!
WHAT'S THAT?
IDIOT—YOU'RE MEANT TO TAKE THE HORSESHOES OFF THE HORSE FIRST!
WHINNY! WHINNY!
BAH! SMIFFY CAN REFEREE THE BOXING INSTEAD!
In school—
I'D LIKE TO BE CHAMPION— I'VE BEEN PRACTISING ON A PUNCH-BAG!
YOU HAVE?
HUH! PUNCH-BAG? IT'S A PAPER-BAG AND YOU CAN'T EVEN PUNCH YOUR WAY THROUGH THAT!
TAP
PAPER
TAP
AMN'T I TOUGH?
WE'LL HAVE AN ELIMINATOR—FATTY AGAINST WILFRED!
I KNOW WHO CAN BE OUR CHAMPION—'ERBERT!
M-ME?
BUT HE'S NOT TOUGH!
So, at the contest—
DOINNG!
I'LL TROUNCE THIS LITTLE CHAPPIE!
REFEREE— WRONG AS USUAL
YOU LOOK A GENTLEMAN— YOU WOULDN'T HIT A CHAP WITH GLASSES, WOULD YOU?
ER—NO! OF COURSE NOT!

CEASE THIS UNRULY BEHAVIOUR INSTANTLY!
In class—
IF YOU MUST FIGHT, YOU SHALL DO SO IN A GENTLEMANLY FASHION IN THE BOXING RING!
I HAVE ARRANGED A MATCH BETWEEN OUR CHAMPION AND A REPRESENTATIVE FROM POSHE STREET ACADEMY.
COO! WHO WILL BE OUR CHAMPION?
Later—
HOW ABOUT ME? I FLOAT LIKE A BUTTERFLY AND STING LIKE A BEE!
YES, AND LOOK LIKE AN APE!
SQUASH!
BONK!
GRR! THAT'S FOR SQUASHING MY CARROT!
OOYAH! WAIL!
LOOKS LIKE PLUG'S BEEN KNOCKED OUT BY A RABBIT PUNCH!
SECONDS OUT!
SCHOOL COOK
SECONDS OUT!
SLURP! I LOVE SECOND HELPINGS!
SCHOOL CANTEEN
ERK! WHERE'S HE GONE?
I THOUGHT NOT! HAR-HAR!
ULK!
HE'LL NEVER BEAT THE COUNT!
But—
DON'T BE TOO SURE—IT COULD BE A LONG TIME TILL SMIFFY COUNTS TO TEN!
ONE—ER—EM—WHAT'S NEXT? IS IT FIVE OR THREE? HARUM!

FOR OLD
Let's take a look at
on whom they would have
If I could be anyone from history I'd be ATTILA THE HUN cos he was tough and mean and nasty and smashed anything which got in his way that's why if I was Attila, I'd make sure Bash Street School got in my way ...
I suppose it might be easier to have been the man who invented steamrollers. He'd have even less bother than that Hun geezer with things that got in his way.
KEEP OUT
IN CASE OF EMERGENCY
Wish I could have been King Henry VIII. He was a well built chap just like myself. I think that was because he had six wives-Must've been great getting six breakfasts, six lunches and six teas! Just a minute-if I had six wives I'd never get in the bathroom in the morning for them putting on their make-up.
MOUNTAINS
HILLS

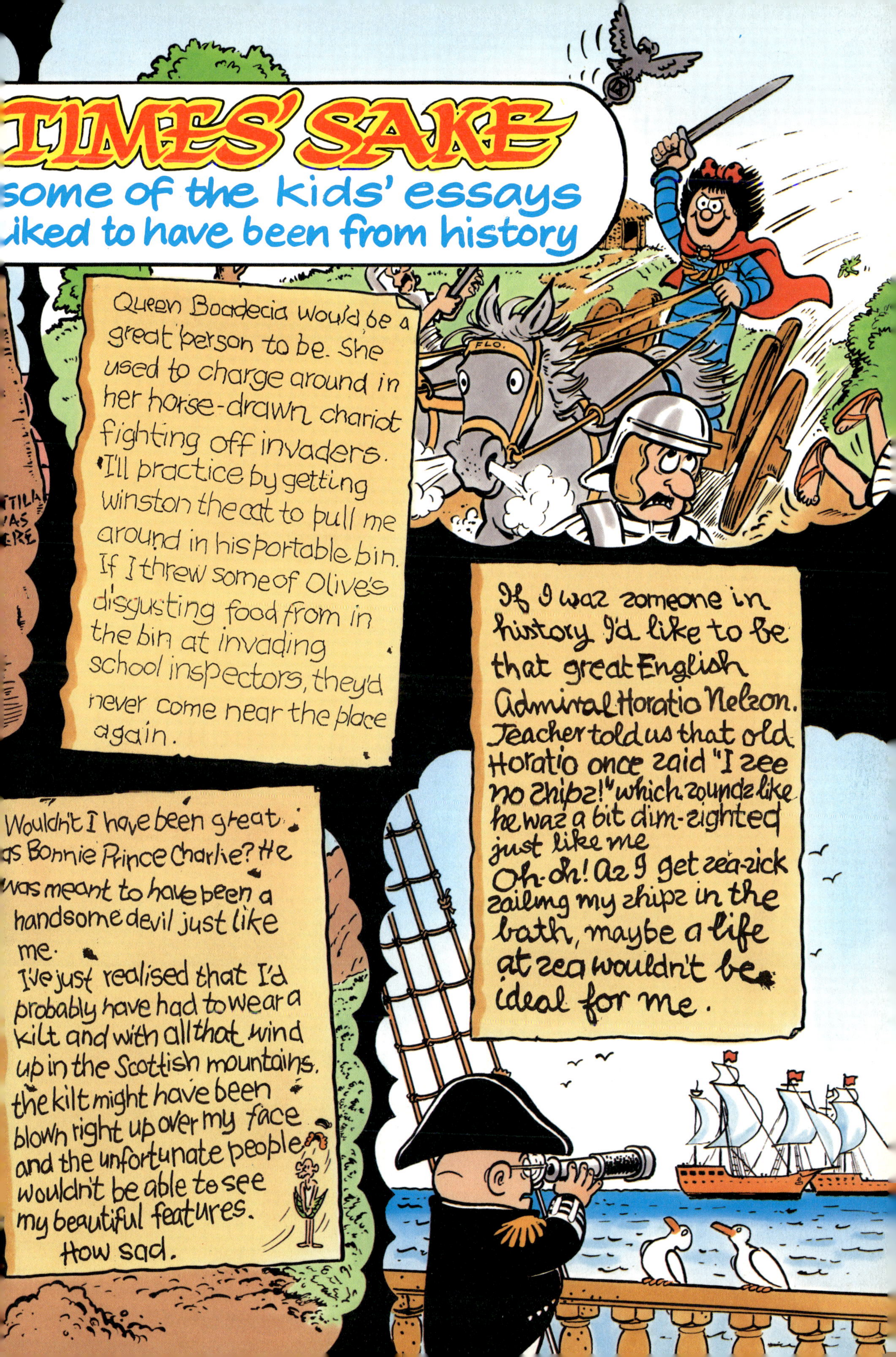

TIMES' SAKE
some of the kids' essays
iked to have been from history
Queen Boadecia would be a great person to be. She used to charge around in her horse-drawn chariot fighting off invaders. I'll practice by getting Winston the cat to pull me around in his portable bin. If I threw some of Olive's disgusting food from in the bin at invading school inspectors, they'd never come near the place again.
FLO.
If I waz someone in history I'd like to be that great English Admiral Horatio Nelzon. Teacher told us that old Horatio once zaid "I zee no zhipz!" which zoundz like he waz a bit dim-zighted just like me. Oh-oh! Az I get zea-zick zailing my zhipz in the bath, maybe a life at zea wouldn't be ideal for me.
Wouldn't I have been great as Bonnie Prince Charlie? He was meant to have been a handsome devil just like me.
I've just realised that I'd probably have had to wear a kilt and with all that wind up in the Scottish mountains, the kilt might have been blown right up over my face and the unfortunate people wouldn't be able to see my beautiful features.
How sad.

DESK JOB
STAND BY FOR DESK INSPECTION.
NO DANGER OF YOU BRINGING TOO MANY BOOKS, SMIFFY — YOU USUALLY FORGET TO BRING YOURSELF!
NOW SEE WHAT YOU'VE DONE! YOU'VE LET MY PET WOODWORMS ESCAPE!
W-WAIT! COUGH! I CAN'T SEE F-FOR ALL THIS SAWDUST! WHAT'S GOING ON?
THUD!
HAMMER!
'BYE, TEACHER!
HEY, COME BACK!
. . . EEK!
TEACHER SAYS I'M DIM — WELL, EVEN I KNEW THAT WOULD HAPPEN TO HIM!
RIGHT! THAT DOES IT! DEAR, SWEET, KIND TEACHER IS ANNOYED!

THAT DESK IS SO FULL OF FOOD IT'S COMING APART AT THE SEAMS . . .
CREAK
. . . JUST LIKE YOU!
SPLUT!
PROD!
TRY TO BRING LESS SCHOOLBOOKS, DEAR BOY — YOU'RE RUINING YOUR DESK.
SIMPER.
FOLLOW ME! I'LL GIVE YOU THE PLANS AND YOU LOT ARE GOING TO MAKE NEW DESKS!
WOODWORK CLASS
THIS SOUNDS TOO MUCH LIKE HARD WORK — SO HERE'S WHAT WE DO . . .
AH, NICE TO SEE THEM ALL WORKING FOR A CHANGE!
PLENTY SAWDUST!
PLANS
ERK! THE LITTLE ROTTERS HAVE NAILED MY SHOES TO THE FLOOR!
CLEVER, EH?
But—
NOT CLEVER ENOUGH — I'M ALWAYS ON GUARD!
ERK!
ONCE YOU FREE ME WE'LL START ON THE NEW DES . . .
THAT'S WHAT HE THINKS.
SAW
HERE ARE THE NEW PLANS!
So—
BAH!
THESE NEW DESKS SHOULD STOP ME HAVING ANY MORE BOTHER! CHORTLE! CHORTLE!

WHAT A CHARMER!

WITH THE BASH STREET PUPS

My Hero
GALES OF LAUGHTER
FOR SMILES ALL YEAR ROUND-GET THE BEANO EVERY WEEK!!

MAKE A

1A

1B

1C

1D

1E

1F

1G

1H

HOW TO DO IT:—

⋆ Trace, on thin card, and colour in all the figures on these two pages. Glue the corresponding halves together (e.g. 1A and 2A) sticking a piece of thread between them from which to hang the completed figure.

⋆ Next, glue the two circles together to form the centrepiece. Using sticky tape fix eight short, plastic straws to the top circle, like the spokes of a wheel (they should stick out a few cms.).

⋆ Now tie the threads from each figure to the end of a separate straw (e.g. Figure A to the end of straw A).

⋆ To complete the mobile, pierce the centre of the circle with the end of a pencil and thread a piece of string (with a knot in one end) through it. Fix the other end of the string to the ceiling or the underside of a shelf and watch the kids moving about in the breeze!

MOBILE

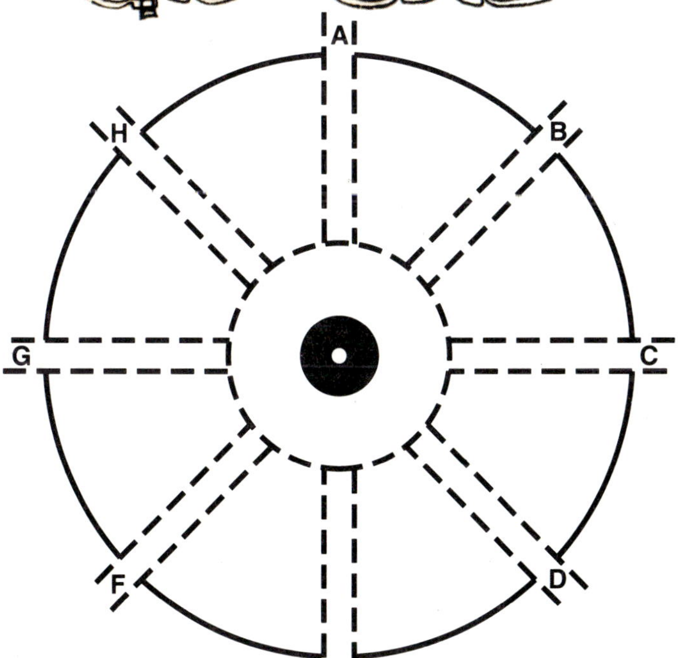

GOOD NATURED FUN
HELLO, KIDDIEWINKS, NATURE STUDY TODAY.
BOO!
AW, NO.
WAAH!
. . . WE'RE ON THE SECOND FLOOR TODAY.
SPOT THE FLAW, DANNY?
YES, THE DESK'S ON IT! OOH! THE AGONY!
Soon—
DON'T WORRY, I KNEW THIS WOULD HAPPEN.
FATTY WILL MAKE A NICE SOFT LANDING FOR US.
OOYAH!
BOUNCE!
BAA!
BLEAT!
BAA!
IMPERSONATING SHEEP. VERY GOOD, CLASS. YAWN.
Much later—
PUFF! WHEEZE!
HE'S GOING TO SLEEP. GASP.

PLOT
MUTTER. PLAN.
I'LL JUST GET THE BOOKS.
WHY ARE THE PUPILS DROPPING WOOD AND PLASTER, ONE WONDERS?
AS I THOUGHT — THEY'RE DIGGING A TUNNEL, THERE'S ONE PROBLEM, THOUGH . . .
BELTS, THIS WAY!
HAR-DE-HAR! THIS IS TOO EASY.
I'LL GO FIRST.
SNAP!
HOWL!
SEE?
I KNEW THIS WOULD HAPPEN, TOO.
EEK!
EEK!
LET'S DO OUR CLASS, CLASS. I DO SO LOVE NATURE.
I'VE GOT A PLOT. TEACHER'S REALLY INTO NATURE, SO —
SNORE! GRUNT!
WHEEZE! PUFF! IT WORKED!
YES, BUT WE'RE SHATTERED.
JUST HAVE A LITTLE SLEEP BEFORE WE ESCAPE. ZZZZZ.
SNORE!
BLAART!
ZZZZZZ!
WOODWORK CLASS? I THOUGHT IT WAS NATURE STUDY TODAY.

LAUGH OLYMPICS
GASP! WHAT'S THIS?
THUNK!
At Bash St. Airport —
I'M HERE, FANS!
SHRIEK!
SWOON!
OLYMPIC TEAM
BASH AIR
WAH!
NOT A VERY GOOD START.
TUG!
THE FIRST EVENT IS MIRROR-SHATTERING!
HMM! IT'S HARD TO PICK A WINNER.
CRACK!
TINKLE!
CRASH!
YOU'RE TOO GOOD FOR US — WE THROW IN THE TOWEL!

IN ATLANTA THEY'RE TRYING OUT "UGLINESS" AS AN EXHIBITION EVENT IN THE OLYMPICS — GUESS WHO'S BEEN PICKED TO REPRESENT BRITAIN!
OLYMPICS
DANNY? WILFRID? 'ERBERT?
SCRATCH!
YOU, YOU FOUL-FEATURED FELLOW!
WHY ME?
SLAP!
THE PILOT MADE ME SIT OUT HERE! I WAS SCARING THE OTHER COMPETITORS!
Back at school —
THIS IS THE LINE-UP FOR THE "UGLINESS" COMPETITION!
LIST
WE HAVE VICTOR VILOVITCH, FROM RUSSIA — DES GUSTING, FROM EIRE — GASTON GHASTLÉ, FROM FRANCE — HANS VON HORRID, FROM GERMANY — AND LAST, BUT NOT LEAST, PLUG, FROM BRITAIN!
SMELLING SALTS
LIST
WAIT! WHAT WAS THAT?
SHATTER!
GASP! HE'S SO UGLY HE'S MANAGED TO SHATTER A MIRROR IN MY HANDBAG!
Flower wilting next —
At the presentation —
IT GIVES ME GREAT PLEASURE . . .
BASH ST SCHOOL
PROUD!
. . . TO COVER UP THESE GHASTLY FACES!
SNIGGER! THAT'S THE MOST UNUSUAL MEDALS CEREMONY WE'VE EVER SEEN!

Super Stooper
REALLY! YOU MUST IMPROVE THEIR POSTURE, TEACHER. THE INSPECTOR'S COMING THIS AFTERNOON.
WHAT DO YOU KNOW ABOUT POSTURE?
BAH! NOT A STRAIGHT BACK IN THE WHOLE CLASS!
Except for Cuthbert Cringeworthy—
LIKE A RAMROD, LADDIE—I'M PROUD OF YOU!
CUTHBERT WILL NOW SHOW YOU HOW TO STAND UP STRAIGHT AND WALK TALL.
IT'S A BOOK OF STAMPS, TEACHER!
GRR! I'LL STAMP ON YOU, PLAIN-FEATURED YOUTH!
Smiffy's wrong as usual—
BOOK, YOU FOOL—NOT BOOT!
SPEAK UP, TEACHER! I CAN'T HEAR YOU FOR THIS BOOT ON MY HEAD!
After lunch—
I MUST GET THESE SLOVENLY SLOUCHERS READY FOR THE INSPECTION—BY JOVE, IS THAT A COIN OF THE REALM?
CLICK!
NO—IT'S A MILK-TOP—YAROOP! MY LUMBAGO!
II

THAT REMINDS ME, TEACHER— I FORGOT TO "POSTURE" FOOTBALL COUPON!
FOOL! GOOD JOB I FORGOT TO FILL IT IN!
YOU MUST CEASE THIS SLOVENLY SLOUCHING. BAH! WHEN I WAS IN THE ARMY, MY BACK WAS LIKE A RAMROD!
LIKE A RAMROD, LADDIE!
SIT UP STRAIGHT!
SEE, IT'S EASY! USE BOOKS. NOW YOU LOT TRY.
Plug does first posture—
WHERE'S YOUR BOOK, LADDIE?
YOU WILL GO HOME AND CLEANSE THOSE GRUBBY JERSEYS AND PRACTISE SITTING UP STRAIGHT FOR THE INSPECTOR'S VISIT.
DING!
A PINCH MORE STARCH, SMIFFY.
OK, TOOTS, AS I WAS SAYING...
STARCH
WASHING MACHINE
THIS IS CLASS IIB, YOUR HIGHNESS. THE TEACHER'S VERY SMART BUT THE PUPILS ARE SLOVENLY.
YOU'VE GOT IT WRONG, HEAD— IT'S A STOOPING TEACHER AND A VERY SMART CLASS!
THE KIDS' JERSEYS ARE OVER-STARCHED
REMIND ME TO GIVE YOU A GOOD STIFF TALKING TO, SMIFFY!
BACK ACHE CREAM
BACK-ACHE PILLS

WHAT A DISPLAY!
I'VE HAD A GREAT IDEA, TEACHER! YOU'RE GOING TO PUT ON A DISPLAY FOR THE KIDS' PARENTS!
WHAT?
PRETTY GOOD, EH?
. . . OHHH!
OOPS!
THUD!
. . . WHAT COMES NEXT?
"SHEEP", EWE SILLY GOAT-ER-KID!
THAT'S IT — BAA, BAA, BLACK GOAT!
PRANG!
SPLUT!
PAIN
. . . TRUANT!
YIKES!
COME BACK, WAYWARD PUPILS!
FAR AWAY

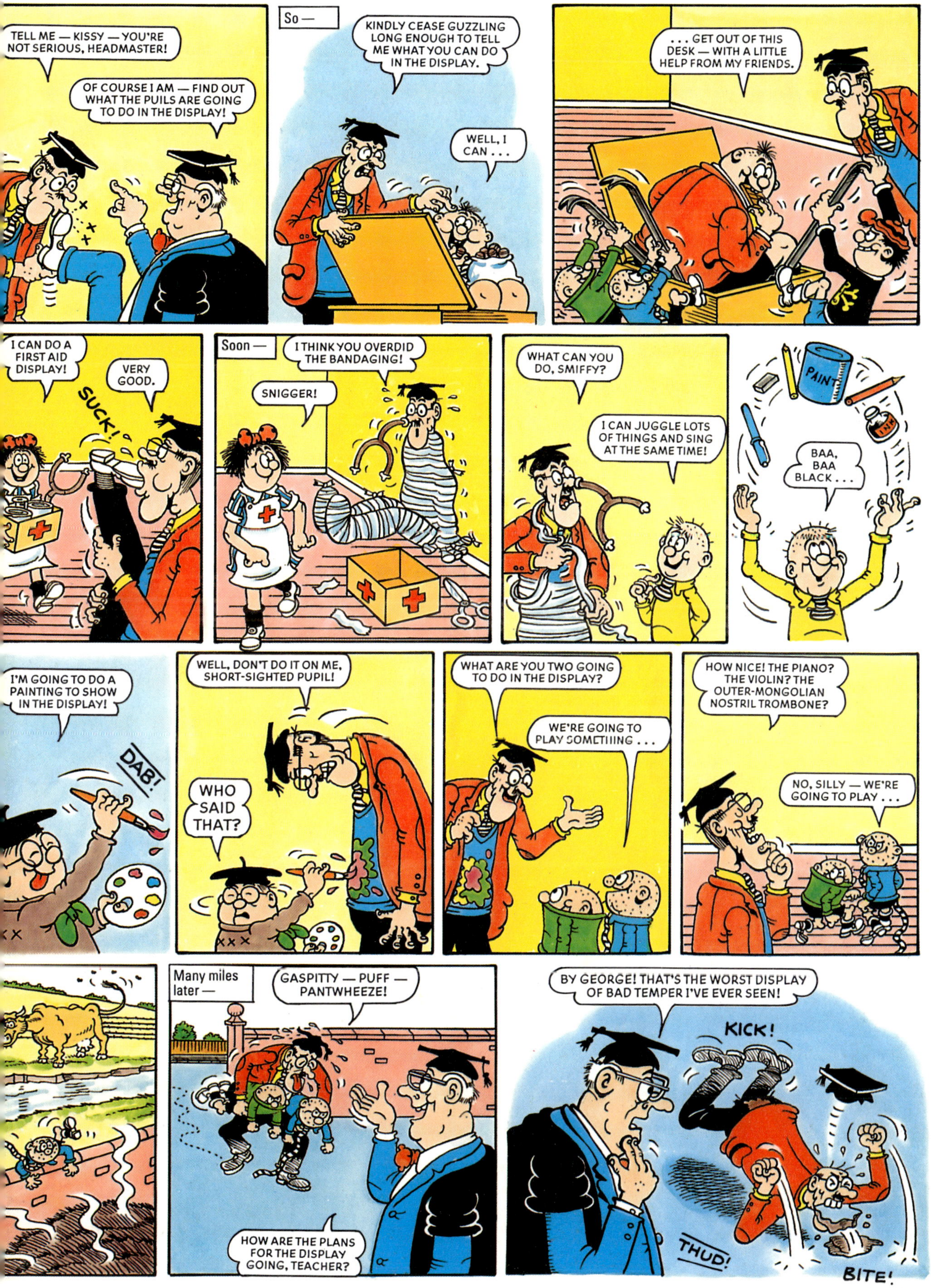
TELL ME — KISSY — YOU'RE NOT SERIOUS, HEADMASTER!
OF COURSE I AM — FIND OUT WHAT THE PUILS ARE GOING TO DO IN THE DISPLAY!
So —
KINDLY CEASE GUZZLING LONG ENOUGH TO TELL ME WHAT YOU CAN DO IN THE DISPLAY.
WELL, I CAN . . .
. . . GET OUT OF THIS DESK — WITH A LITTLE HELP FROM MY FRIENDS.
I CAN DO A FIRST AID DISPLAY!
VERY GOOD.
SUCK!
Soon —
I THINK YOU OVERDID THE BANDAGING!
SNIGGER!
WHAT CAN YOU DO, SMIFFY?
I CAN JUGGLE LOTS OF THINGS AND SING AT THE SAME TIME!
PAINT
BAA, BAA BLACK . . .
I'M GOING TO DO A PAINTING TO SHOW IN THE DISPLAY!
DAB!
WELL, DON'T DO IT ON ME, SHORT-SIGHTED PUPIL!
WHO SAID THAT?
WHAT ARE YOU TWO GOING TO DO IN THE DISPLAY?
WE'RE GOING TO PLAY SOMETHING . . .
HOW NICE! THE PIANO? THE VIOLIN? THE OUTER-MONGOLIAN NOSTRIL TROMBONE?
NO, SILLY — WE'RE GOING TO PLAY . . .
Many miles later —
GASPITTY — PUFF — PANTWHEEZE!
HOW ARE THE PLANS FOR THE DISPLAY GOING, TEACHER?
BY GEORGE! THAT'S THE WORST DISPLAY OF BAD TEMPER I'VE EVER SEEN!
KICK!
THUD!
BITE!

WHAT A WAY TO SLEIGH!
KISS ME
ALL OUR CHRISTMAS PRESENTS ARE READY TO DELIVER.
JUST A MINUTE — WHERE'S SMIFFY?
RIP!
THIS'LL DO NICELY.
LIKE MY CLOAK? NOW ALL I NEED IS A BEARD.
HMM!
SCHOOL
THAT'S THE SLEIGH TAKEN CARE OF.
Then —
SNIP!
HMM! I THINK WE CAN ARRANGE THE REINDEER TOO.
TOSS
TOSS
WHAP!
THUD!

Then —
WHAT'S THIS?
YOU WRAP THE GIFT, TWIT — NOT YOURSELF!
RIP!
LET'S DELIVER THE GIFTS IN TRADITIONAL STYLE.
OK!
SCHOOL NURSE
EEK!
I N-NEED A NURSE.
TA, NURSE.
COTTON WOOL
GREAT BEARD, BUT WHAT ABOUT A SLEIGH AND SOME REINDEER.
Soon —
HO-HO-HO! OFF, WE GO!
GLOW
SNIGGER! SO THAT'S WHY THEY WANTED THOSE BRANCHES.
P-PRESENTS FOR US? HOW KIND!
DONG!
HOW ROTTEN! THE HORRORS!
THEY'VE GIVEN US ALL THEIR SCHOOL EQUIPMENT!
THAT'S WHAT THEY THINK! HERE ARE THEIR REAL GIFTS! MERRY CHRISTMAS, READERS!
WINSTON
TEACHER
HEAD

HURDLING
GREAT PRACTICE ON MY PAPER ROUND!
PLONK
DANNY
LEAP
ASTRONOMY
I'VE DISCOVERED A NEW PLANET!
'ERBERT
SWIVEL